SCARS

VICTORIA AMIDOU

Scars

By

Victoria Amidou

P.O. Box 085137

Racine, Wisconsin 53408

www.victoriaamidou.com

All Rights Reserved. This book or parts may not be reproduced in any form, stored in a retrieval system or transmitted in any form by any means-electronic, mechanical, photocopy, recording or otherwise- without written permission of the publisher, except as provided by United States of America copyright law.

Copyright © 2017 by Victoria Amidou

Published in the United States of America 2017

ISBN – 13: 978-0-692-95278-8

ISBN – 10: 0692952780

CONTENTS

TITLE PAGE..
CONTENTS...
ACKNOWLEDGMENTS ....
INTRODUCTION ....
  « CHAPTER 1 ABRASIONS » 1
  « CHAPTER 2 BRUISED AND BROKEN » 13
  « CHAPTER 3 CUTS »..19
  « CHAPTER 4 DEFACED BY DEJA VU » 25
  « CHAPTER 5 EROSION » 35
  « CHAPTER 6 FRACTURES » 43
  « CHAPTER 7 GASH »...55
  « CHAPTER 8 HEMORRHAGE »..........................61
  « CHAPTER 9 INCISIONS » 69
  « CHAPTER 10 JAGGED » 79
  « CHAPTER 11 KELOIDS » 85
  « CHAPTER 12 LESIONS » 93
  « CHAPTER 13 MAIMED».................................105
  « CHAPTER 14 NICKS » 111
  « CHAPTER 15 OPPROBRIUM » 117
  « CHAPTER 16 PUNCTURE » 125
  « CHAPTER 17 QUESTIONS » 131
  « CHAPTER 18 REMNANT » 143
  « CHAPTER 19 SCRATCH » 153
  « CHAPTER 20 TATTOO »..................................167
  « CHAPTER 21 UNDERLYING » 173
  « CHAPTER 22 VITIATE » 179
  « CHAPTER 23 WOUNDED »..............................185
  « CHAPTER 24 X MARKS THE SPOT »..............193
  « CHAPTER 25 YOU »..203
  « CHAPTER 26 ZERO IN ON TARGET » 213

« CHAPTER 27 PHYSICAL EXTERNAL »............................ 223
« CHAPTER 28 PHYSICAL INTERNAL » 233
« CHAPTER 29 EXTERNAL SPIRIT » 243
« CHAPTER 30 INTERNAL SPIRIT » 249

APPENDIX ....

NOTES ....

LINKS ....

OVERVIEW ....

AUTHOR ....

POEM ....

ACKNOWLEDGMENTS

There once was a time when I thought that thanking oneself was sacrilege but that was when I didn't have a clue as to who Victoria was to herself. In the infant stages of discovering me I quickly learned that it is a must and that it is true spiritual-ness for me. It is the highest form of respect to give thanks to oneself.

To acknowledge the God of you by acknowledging the God in you. So, I take this moment to acknowledge Victoria Amidou for soaring with scars. I also take this moment to give thanks to all of my love ones who weathered the storms with me and chose to love me to life because of who I AM!

To Ishmeal Amponsah, the One who completes me, I dedicate this book to you for you are my inspiration. Without you none of this would be possible because you are my all in all, the air that I breathe, the other part of me. When I dream it is you that's there. When I envision the rest of this journey it is your presence that is felt. It is my honor to acknowledge the continuous flow of oneness that bonds us for you are my Divine. I embrace all that is to come for us as we continue this journey fused in complete Godliness. I thank you for encouraging me to be who I am without boundaries, without limits, and within love.

INTRODUCTION

Statistics show that over 50 million people have scars, whether formed purposely or by accident. Scars be it self-inflicted or by the hands of someone else leaves you changed forever.

It doesn't matter that the wound is closed and healed. Healing doesn't mean that you come out without scars.

There are some wounds that leave you damaged above and below the surface. Yes, technically you've healed. However, healed doesn't equate to being the same. A wound even healed can still be the cause of great pain and agony. Be it physical, psychological, or spiritual and sometimes all three simultaneously.

Some scars are so profound that they are a constant reminder of the trauma that you've experienced, so much so that even others can see and even feel them.

There are those among us that even wear their scars as a badge of honor while others wear them as a badge of shame.

No matter the reason nor the cause I disagree with the statistics. I know that every person on this planet in some form or another has scars and are in some form or another trying within their means to deal with them.

« CHAPTER 1 ABRASIONS »

It has come to my realization that scars have a significant meaning in our lives, meaning far beyond what we deem to be relevant.

Most in our society tend to look at scars negatively because of what they have been exposed to by others. It is that early exposure that hinders us in all areas of our lives.

We are oftentimes shaped and molded based on someone else's belief system and experiences when we first arrive in this realm.

Being in the physical infant stage leaves us vulnerable to the experiences of our first teachers. The ones who are set to be our caregivers and loved ones.

It is a sad reality that most of us didn't enter this earth realm being welcomed by conscious people. Their awareness was not that of holiness because they weren't given the tools required to cultivate what was inside of them upon entry into this earth realm.

Even when they became aware that they were of greatness they still did nothing to cultivate the gift and used the excuses, "I'm afraid and I don't know how!"

Which, don't get me wrong, it was their truth. However, be it truth or not, it was still not a valid reason to not even try.

They were so paralyzed by their fear that they allowed it to hinder their purpose on this planet and aimlessly wondered from one religion to another trying to find meaning. Even looking for what they considered to be their purpose.

Most never coming to the realization that their meaning and purpose was always within them. They did not have to go searching outside of themselves for it.

So, in doing so they wounded themselves and eventually created their scars. A manifestation of spiritual, psychological, and physical abuse. Self-inflicted, mind you.

It is the rough rubbing of yourselves that leave abrasions on not only the body but also the mind as well as the spirit.

Treating yourselves in a manner that is not befitting to that of a GOD. Callously handling yourselves and then turning around and having the audacity to think that the next person will treat you with tender loving care when you don't.

The gentle treatment of yourselves is a must. You must learn how to be gentle with you and that's in every area of your existence.

Stop asking people to do for you what you are not willing to do for yourself. It is you that set the standard for your own treatment.

When those abrasive thoughts come into your mind you must find a healthy way to release them for that moment.

I say for that moment because what works for you today may not work for you tomorrow because you are evolving.

It is this constant state of change that enables you to become a better you. When you resist change you cheat yourself. You hinder the purpose for your life.

There are moments when having these abrasions will work for your benefit. Yes, they will. See, it is the pain from the roughness that will allow you to see what you no longer want in your life.

You will learn from the unnecessary roughness that you don't want to feel that way because it is painful. You will then begin to teach yourself not to do that again.

You will also learn that even the smallest abrasions can have the biggest impact on your life. These abrasions can leave you with permanent scars as well.

These scars are a constant reminder that you weren't gentle with yourself nor did you set the standard for others to be gentle with you. If you have allowed someone else to see how you cause unnecessary roughness to yourself, then what makes you think that they will treat you any differently.

You tend to think that others are supposed to do for you what you are not willing to do for yourselves. Lies you tell.

It is not the responsibility of the next person to treat you any better than you treat yourself. Although it is an honor to have someone who would make that kind of sacrifice for you.

Abrasive behavior leaves behind psychological scars that are not quickly identified because it can be easily hidden.

Those who have psychological scars tend to be the greatest pretenders. They learn very early on to mask the pain that comes from those scars.

They smile in the presence of others even when they feel like crying. They walk around pretending that the pain from the scars aren't real. Saying to themselves, **"it's just in my mind."**

They even go so far as to rationalize the pain from the scars and how they received them. They also flip the scenario around and say that what was wrong is now right. That the maltreatment of themselves is not maltreatment. That the harsh and rough treatment of their physical, psychological, and spiritual selves is good. Knowing deep down that it is a lie.

They try to numb the pain from the scars by self-medicating. They begin to use alcohol and illicit drugs to temporarily relieve themselves of the pain.

There are even moments where psychologically they fool themselves into thinking that the pain is pleasure. So, they go about seeking out ways to cause themselves even more pain as a way of release.

The mind becomes a battle field between reality and fantasy. They begin to fantasize about the way in which the scars happen. Yes, even surface scars can cause psychological damage.

Everyone's mindset is different and what one being can easily handle can be catastrophic to the next.

Those unnecessary rough moments be it thought or deed need to be immediately handled before it gets out of control.

There are methods that you can use to bring those thoughts and or deeds under submission by allowing your spirit to take the lead in your life.

You allowing your spirit to guide and direct your path will bring about greater clarity in your life.

By stopping and examining why you do what you do and why you think what you think and then slowly and gently feeling the pain and asking your spirit to redirect that negative energy and to show you how to change that which is negative into a positive.

The scars from the abrasions will always be there and in some instances, so will the pain but do not be dismayed. You can learn how to cope and live with the pain without any further damage to your trinity.

There must come a defining moment in your life when you must make the choice to do better for you. Not for anyone else. You and you alone are responsible for your treatment of you. Just as only you know what feels good verses what feels bad for you.

Don't allow anyone to rub you the wrong way and tell you that it feels good.

You must learn to give yourself permission to receive what is required to start your process of healing. No one on this planet can do that for you.

The necessary steps can be taught to you but the willingness to start and keep going must come from you.

Those rough layers from the abrasions must be treated gently. It is a part of the process to recovering what was lost and damaged.

Although the abrasions happened in an instant it may take a lifetime to recover.

Acceptance is one of the first necessary keys to this recovery process. You must learn to be honest with yourself at all costs. Remember your truth to you also determines other people's truth to you. Again, you can't get what you don't give.

There must be within you a willingness to accept that kindness on your part is needed from you. No matter the situation nor circumstance, unnecessary roughness is never ever allowed because once the damage is done it is done.

No one knows the full extent of what is being felt but you and it is you and only you that must do the work necessary for the healing and dealing with the issue at hand. No one and I mean absolutely no one should be treating you better than you are treating you.

For it is you and you alone that has been and will always be with you, no matter how many people are around, so get use to handling you with tender loving care.

You must come to a place where you are comfortable loving you from the deepest part of self. Loving you is a direct representation of how you treat yourself. Don't confuse wearing designer clothes and driving expensive cars with loving you because those are material things. I am talking about core loving, where you are attentive to what you eat, drink, and feed your spirit.

Are you taking good care of you?

Do you like what you feel when you think of just you?

What do you think when you are alone?

Ask yourself, why do you do the things that you do?

What makes you like what you like?

What makes you choose what you choose?

Who are you?

Do you even know?

See these questions although simple are very important to your healing.

Abrasions start long before you communicate them where others around you can over-stand. It is the under-standing and the miscommunication skills that hinder you in the early stages of development after birth which causes further abrasions to an already damaged being.

Birth is painful for both mother and child. It leaves both scarred in one way or another while the primary source of concern as far as pain, is given to the mother, the child is not often considered, pain wise that is.

It is the assurance that the child is born alive and healthy by societies standards. However, society doesn't take into consideration what the child has undergone during the birthing process. It is assumed that since the child shows no signs to them of being damaged, that all is well.

Very few talk about the trauma of childbirth from the child's prospective. The child can't articulate effectively what they have undergone during this process.

Babies are born with crying as their primary source of verbal communication. So, for them to have their needs met you must learn to differentiate between their cries.

It is here where babies experience more abrasions due to the parents or caregivers lack of proper communication with the child. In the adults mind they think because the child is in infancy that they do not think on a certain level. Never thinking that the child has a spirit that is not in the infancy stage. The spirit is housed in the body of the infant and must adhere to the rules and guidelines set in place when that entry point was chosen.

The spirit is in constant spiritual contact with the body and is doing what is required to ensure that the body gets what is needed to survive.

The child is at a disadvantage because they lack the necessary verbal skills to articulate that to the adult in a way in which they will over-stand without frustration. It is this frustration that causes the child to cry out. Babies come equipped with thoughts far beyond what their parents know. They just can't say it with words.

They use body language to communicate with their caregivers, hoping that they will pick up on the settle cues. This is done long before frustration sets in.

Even societies normal babies receive abrasions by their caregivers unbeknownst to the caregiver. Cultures and traditions have placed damaging mindsets on caregivers long before they begin to procreate.

It is these ideals, beliefs, and customs that leave embedded deep within, the preconceived notions that certain things are right when in fact they are wrong.

A quick example is the notion that you can spoil a baby by holding them too much. Which is simply not true.

Babies require the hue-man touch. Having been in their mother's womb for nine months being constantly caressed, carried, nurtured, pampered, and cared for by her body. So, what makes some think once the baby is born that they no longer require the same. Especially after the birthing experience which I stated before is abrasive to both the mother and child.

It is a fact that the child needs your reassurance, even more so after birth because of the uncertainty of the world that they have been birth into.

It is traumatic and stressful to the child who is trying to cope with being in this realm and being detached from the maternal life force as they have known it to be.

They have gone from being constantly valued to being devalued. Left to cry for affection and attention.

Left to being propped up with a bottle and told, "I am not going to spoil you." As if they were some leftovers with the potential of being left out too long.

These early childhood abrasions will result in deep penetrating scars if not treated properly. It is the mismanagement of the surface wounds that cause the infections and it is the mismanaged infections that cause the scars.

SCARS • 12

The manifestation of all things whether positive or negative come from you.

« CHAPTER 2 BRUISED AND BROKEN »

Bruises are caused by trauma to the skin. An injury that was sustained causing the tiny blood vessels to rupture. These tiny blood vessels are called capillaries. Once these capillaries rupture the blood within them leaks out thus causing a bruise just beneath the skins surface. There are many causes of trauma that create bruises.

Trauma however don't just cause bruises to the skin, they also cause bruises to the mind and spirit. The outer body has received only surface trauma but there is trauma so deep that the outer body sometimes isn't even aware that it even exists. The body has been functioning with the bruises so long that it thinks that the trauma from the bruising is normal.

We as hue-man beings are so great at creating that we sometimes aren't even aware that we are doing it. Especially when the creating is negative. We tend to give ourselves credit for the positive aspects of creating but lay the total blame on others when it comes to the negative. The truth of the matter is, all aspects of our lives were and is being created by us.

You are a very powerful being and all that you seek is right within you. No outside source is more powerful than you are when it comes to your life. You are and have always been the creative force behind all things you, be it negative or positive.

The unfortunate aspects of negative creating causes trauma that leaves behind bruising. Some of which can't be seen, but in the beginning, can definitely be felt. There are times when the pain becomes a constant part of the daily living that you become preconditioned to accept it as normal.

Each individual on this planet has been bruised knowingly and unknowingly. No matter how short or long the life span.

The categorizing of trauma still doesn't negate the fact that it has happen and it doesn't matter if it is coming directly from you or indirectly from you, it still needs to be dealt with.

It is the direct trauma coming from you that is worse than the indirect trauma because with direct trauma you are keenly aware that you are causing it. It is your direct intent to cause yourself harm.

Fixing the brokenness is essential to the success of your mission and the only way to do that is by being totally honest with yourself about what caused the brokenness in the first place.

The body is quick to deny responsibility of any wrong doing to self. Therefore, acknowledging the wrong and the root cause of it is the first steps to fixing the brokenness.

Just because you are broken doesn't mean that you are defeated. There is always a chance to mend before the end.

The necessary steps to mending are etched within the fabric of your spirit being. That's why tapping into the inner most parts of yourself are essential to this healing process.

When the healing process has begun you will encounter people who are important players in your healing process. These people will force you to look at yourself in a way that you never have before.

They will anger and frustrate you with the things that are vital to the change that needs to take place in order to fix the brokenness.

They will be the very things that annoy you about yourself and this will cause you to take a closer look at the person you are on the outside. Once the outside examination is done then you will start looking at the inner you.

You will begin to ask yourself why, when, and how questions. These questions will be relevant to your mending process and once the answers start coming you will then begin to realize that you and you alone caused the damage.

You will start to think negatively about the answers and yourself before you see the positive aspects of the answers and their relevance to your mending.

The doubt is natural and you must train yourself to see pass it. The focus at this point should be on the evolution of your physical self in order to allow your spiritual self to lead.

You will also wonder how did you allow yourself to get to the point of brokenness especially since you knew better. This too is natural and it is okay to feel this way just make sure you do not stay in this feeling.

Give ownership to whatever you are feeling because it is important to validate your feelings so that you can empty out that space for something new. This is also cleansing for both the spirit and the body.

In your brokenness, along with everything else, you have also become a terrorist to yourself and with every passing day that you refuse to start the mending process, you further terrorize yourself.

There is an unfortunate truth that comes along with you terrorizing yourself and that is the possibility of you terrorizing others depending on the depth of your brokenness that is.

You must also over-stand that the level of your brokenness depends on the level of your refusal to comply with your spirit.

While in your repairing stage of your brokenness you will begin to notice that you have been allowing certain things to happen to you that you knew would cause you more pain.

You purposely chose people who would inflict pain upon you, this pain, you subconsciously deemed necessary. You wanted someone other than yourself to validate your unworthiness by inflicting a greater degree of pain than what you inflicted upon yourself. You feel unworthy of the gift that God has given you and the path that has been chosen for you is intimidating. So, you try to do things that will cancel out the gift, not knowing that there is nothing that you can do to cancel what God has already chosen for you to do. It will be achieved, no matter how many life times it takes.

You will do what is required of you because giving up is not an option.

« CHAPTER 3 CUTS »

Cuts don't have to be physical. The choices that you make can bring about deep psychological cuts that scar you for life. These cuts can range from surface to deep. Even the surface cuts can still cause trauma that can permanently damage you in multiple ways.

Sometimes it is the surface cuts that cause the greatest pain, sending shockwaves throughout your entire body. Oftentimes these cuts are unintentional.

It is the unintentional cuts that surprise you the most. These cuts oftentimes come when you are doing something that you deem to be good. You know, the things that take very little effort or energy. The usual everyday stuff and then the unexpected happens. A slip up and then boom, you cut yourself.

Now what happens when your physical cuts require you to cut people and things out of your life? There are times when the cuts alter you temporarily but then there are those cuts that are so deep that it alters you permanently, so much so that your life as you knew it changes forever.

The pain of these cuts whether surface or deep causes trauma and that trauma affects the way you deal with others. The trauma from these cuts no matter the depth leaves you wondering, why?

Yes, you know that you have been cut and you may even know how but the why of the matter is troubling to you and even when you try to rationalize it there is still so much left to analyze.

You even play the events over and over again in your mind to see if it was anything that you could have done to prevent it from happening and to see if it was totally your fault. No matter the reason and who's to blame the damage has already been done and now it is up to you to decide how you are going to deal with it.

What is your next course of action?

How do you intend to cope with the damage that has been left behind?

What is the lesson that you learned from the events that caused the cuts in the first place?

Sometimes little or no thought goes into the aftermath. Typically, after such trauma most are on auto mode doing what is natural and not considering the spiritual aspects of the events nor what is required to effectively deal with the damage so that there is little or no permanent scars left behind.

There are some events that lead to cuts that are actually meant to make things better in order to heal the damage that was created.

Certain events are meant to cut people and even things out of your life to help you and not to hurt you. It may not seem like it in the beginning because of the pain that is involved.

We are preconditioned to think that all pain leads to the road of negativity when in fact some pain is needed in order to let you know that something is wrong. It is the spirits cry to the body to adhere and the bodies cry to you for help.

The pain is the indicator that something is wrong and that it needs to be fixed. The pain has a purpose and when you listen and find out where the source of the pain is coming from then you can do what is required to fix it.

If you would just stop and take an inventory of what is happening in your life and listen to your inner you then you can save yourself a world of pain. When you treat the source of your pain early then the likelihood of permanent damage is slim to none.

See, it is the crying out of the spirit to be allowed to lead that's causing your body to malfunction and this also is causing the pain. This pain must be dealt with, although some pain must be felt in order to heal.

SCARS • 22

In order to walk into your destiny, you must learn to walk in pain. You must learn that some pain must be felt in order to push you into your purpose.

There are times when you hesitate to do what is required and there are times when the spirit will allow a cut to get you to stop and pay attention to what is to come, to redirect you, to reposition you. You must be in the right place at the right time in order for certain things to happen in your life that are ordained by God. So, because of your unwillingness to comply the spirit will push you by allowing certain events to happen in order to get you where you need to be.

There comes a time when you must make the necessary cuts in order to continue on the path that was chosen for you. Certain things and people are a hindrance to the development of your purpose. If you continue to allow these people and things to reign in your life the pain that you have already received will continue to mount to the point of unbearability.

You will even have to cut out certain behaviors as well because certain types of behaviors are not allowed as you continue your journey. The purpose for which you were chosen is far greater than any amount of pain that you must endure and even as you excel in your journey some pain will never go away.

Some scars from the cuts must remain as a constant reminder to you so that you will not do whatever caused the cuts in the first place to happen again. Although the scars remain they will not stop you from achieving what God has chosen for you. You will achieve your goals with the scars.

You will walk in your purpose scarred, battered, and bruised but victorious because some cuts are necessary for your growth, development, and healing.

Always remember that even if your cut is deep and surface scars remain, you will still walk into your purpose no matter the pain. You are anointed to achieve certain things and nothing will hinder you as long as you do what is required.

Your cuts are essential, even the ones that are seemingly done by accident because everything is to guide you to what you were chosen for.

So, don't fret over the people and things that had to be cut out of your life because they weren't meant to go with you. They served their purpose and are no longer needed. You must learn that certain cutting is mandatory because nothing is to interfere with what God has chosen for you.

There comes a point when you must differentiate between purposeful and non-purposeful cutting. Even if the cutting is a physical cut on the body or within the body there is still purpose in it, same as the cutting out of certain things and people.

As useful as the umbilical cord is, at the appropriate time, it still must be cut.

« CHAPTER 4 DEFACED BY DEJA VU »

The black man has been preconditioned to run from and devalue the black woman when she has awakened from her slumber.

When the black woman has truly begun her journey to recognizing her spiritual self that is when she becomes the biggest threat to all and I mean all.

No one who is still in the sleeping period wants to deal with a black woman who recognizes and adheres to the spirit that dwells within her.

When a black woman reaches this point in her journey she is lethal. Her mouth and movements become calculated. It is at this moment where a boy masquerading as a man becomes defensive and resentful towards her.

It is also here where she will become isolated and sometimes even lonely in a room full of people. She now knows that she has been fooled into believing the untruths that have been told to her all of her life.

Her movements become strategic and meticulous. She begins to analyze all things that seem ordinary. If in a relationship her man becomes the subject of her research of self. She wants to know what caused her to choose this man, especially if he is not up to her current standards.

It is a given that the average black woman is ahead of the average black man in most areas. So, when a black woman is with a black man who fails to even try to keep up, it's a turn off.

The black woman knows that she must work harder at being her, more so than any other woman on this planet because of who she is, whether she is aware of it or not.

When the actual awakening process starts to happen, initially she is confused and even frustrated because she is not truly ready for what has begun.

Praying for something and being ready for it is two different things.

At all times, we must know our self.

The black man has been programmed to desert the black woman emotionally, physically, and spiritually. He has a warped view of who she is and how she must be handled. He doesn't view her as his equal and surely not as his superior. So, she is handled as an unequal and inferior being.

The unawaken black man once he realizes that the black woman he is with has awakened begins to show signs of envy and hatred toward the black woman. This is where he starts to disrespect, demean, and devalue her.

This is his effort to make her revert to the slumber stage. Unfortunately, once the awakening process starts nothing and no one can stop it. Nevertheless, unbeknownst to the black man he still tries.

The black man notices the changes in the black woman, he is just not aware as to what exactly is causing the changes and this makes him uncomfortable.

In this stage of discomfort, the black man will be left wondering why the black woman no longer seeks attention and compliments from him. He may even assume that she is cheating because in his mind there is no way she can be making these changes on her own.

It is also at this stage where the black woman will start to focus more on the inner her than the outer her. Her time will be used more wisely and she will

start to value herself more. It is here that she realizes that the most important person in her life is her and that this realization doesn't make her feel guilty. She walks different now that she is more important to herself than anyone else and that it is not selfish but necessary.
This necessary importance of the black woman to herself is paramount to the forthcoming changes that she must make. She must become aware of herself in a way that welcomes the necessary changes instead of resenting them.

During this process, she must remain focused because those closest to her will be her unwelcomed distractions. They will try with everything in them to stop her from achieving her goal.

The awakening process requires work and plenty of it and it will take the rest of her life to stay awake.

This spiritual awakening will remove some people from your life, some you thought would always be there and it will bring some people in your life that you never thought possible. No matter who goes or who comes you must keep in mind that no one is allowed to become more important to you than you.

You are and have always been the most vital part of your life and at this moment I will tell you that it is a must that you put yourself first in all things.

Don't allow the fear of self to stop you from doing what is required to be the you that God has intended for you to be.

Learn to love yourself in a way that embraces your individuality and uniqueness because it is the fear of self that has you conforming to someone else's idea of beauty.

You must learn to accept the true you and not the assembly line version. Being true to the spirit that dwells within you allows the body to be at peace and harmony while on this planet.

It is the acknowledgment and adherence of the oneness that keeps you from the snares and traps of the negative forces that linger around you.

You wanting to be someone else is a great disservice to you and your creator because it is your uniqueness that is needed to do what you have been chosen to do by God.

When you continue to allow the forces outside of you to control the way you treat yourself, negativity is sure to follow.

It is the studying of self that is sure to lead you to a victorious life on this planet. When you learn who you are, devaluing yourself to fit in with others no longer is an issue for you. When you begin to walk in the true you, you will no longer seek fake friendships and fake connections with toxic people.

The fake and toxic people are coming to you because you are their magnet. Yes, you are attracting what you are to yourself.

So, when you stop being fake and toxic to yourself your magnet effect changes. You are the change that you seek. It is not the people around you that need to change, it is you.

You have become so comfortable pretending to be something and someone that you're not, so much so that you no longer accept the fact that is not the true you.

Your spirit has been sending you signals and warnings but you refuse to adhere. You have been tricked into thinking that this is the right way to be.

You no longer want to be true to yourself because of the work that's required to do so will force you to come face to face with the true you. The you that was chosen to be greater than the fake you. The you that over-stands her purpose and why she was chosen.

The you that respects the body that she uses and respects the spirit that she houses and knows that she must allow the two to work together to achieve the task that was given to her.

She must accept the fact that the spirit must lead at all times and that the spirit existed before the body and that submitting to the higher being is paramount in order to achieve oneness.

Your quest is to become what you seek. You seek the ultimate love, then you must become the ultimate love. Yes! You must love yourself in a way that draws the very same to you.

You must learn to think, feel, and be what you seek and don't allow anyone or anything to sway you away from what is important to your purpose.

Do everything with you in mind. Take all the necessary steps to ensure your survival first. Then everything else will follow. You are the most important person in your life, now start treating yourself as such. I will keep saying it until you comprehend it.

This is not about narcissism nor selfishness, this is about oneness. The completeness of self. When this is achieved you will no longer feel cheated, angry, hurt, or bitter.

You will then begin the process of forgiving the body for not allowing the spirit to lead. You will look at all things differently and accept responsibility for all the things you have allowed to happen in your life whether advertently or inadvertently.

Your healing begins the moment you take full responsibility for being the creator of all things you and when I say all things you I am speaking of the things that have happened in your adult life that has either helped or harmed you in some way.

It is through your thoughts and or deeds that have or have not brought to you the things that you have or have not wanted.

You are far more powerful than you think. You are your creator when you step into this realm. You have the power to make or break yourself.

You have and will always be the one in control of self. You allow what you want or don't want in your life by first thinking it, then secondly feeling it, and then thirdly carrying it out. It is the law of attraction.

You must learn to control what you are thinking and feeling before it is created. You have a small window of opportunity during this thinking and feeling process before it gets to the creation stage.

Whatever you give your energy to is what you will create. You will manifest the strongest and most powerful force at that given moment. Whether it be love or hate, you create it with what you think and feel.

Now, close your eyes and take several slow deep breaths and think about every life altering event that has taken place in your life to this date and now think about what you were thinking and feeling at that moment. Be honest with yourself.

Did you think and or feel any of that happening before it actually happened?

Did you sense something was wrong or off and refused to adhere to the feeling within?

You must learn to accept responsibility for all things you. It is that intuition that drives you to listen and you dismissed it. You even go as far as to say that you are over reacting. Oh, and I like this one. "It's just my past". No, it's not just your past, it's your present gifting you with foresight and it's warning you of what is to come, if you don't adhere.

The spirit that you house has not limits nor an age. Your spirit knows what your body doesn't and therefore sends you messages to keep you safe so the mission that the spirit was sent here to accomplish can be completed without interruptions or delays.

Even the moments of déjà vu that you often have are glimpses of what has already happen. Events in which the spirit has already taken part in, although you have yet to experience in the body or natural in this lifetime.

When you start to experience moments of déjà vu don't be afraid or try to stop it because it is during these moments of déjà vu that your spirit is sending you clues as to what is next for you. All you have to do during those moments are to (if you're in a safe place) close your eyes and take slow deep breaths and allow the déjà vu moment to play itself out. Once the moment is complete you will feel a great sense of relief and oftentimes answers that you have been seeking will be revealed during those moments.

You must always remember that you are the one in control and that you are the creator of the things that happen to you in this realm.

Simply put, you have the power!

« CHAPTER 5 EROSION »

Erosion is the slow wearing a way of your mind and body as a result of the things you have been doing. It doesn't matter whether it was purposeful or not. It is the way that you treat yourself while on this planet that will determine how slow or how fast your erosion process will take.

Age, diet, and how well you treat yourself are all indicators of whether the signs of erosion will show and when.

Before conception erosion has started to take place, long before your parents even met one another. It is the things that they have done and allowed to happen to their bodies that have scarred the reproductive organs and systems. The sperm cells are affected by the things that the male puts into his body and by his daily activities, just as the uterus and the ovaries are in the female.

Once the sperm cell penetrates the egg everything that the male and female has done combines. The joining of the two has created you, you are inheriting 50 percent of your chromosomes from the male and 50 percent from the female.

So, everything that your parents have done has for better or worse altered their reproductive system and this can lead to psychological and physical erosions.

The dis-eases the you have are more than likely hereditary. A lot of studies have place the main blame on that of the mother while oftentimes the father gets away free of blame.

The female must do extensive research on the male before procreation, to learn as much about him and his family as she can. It is this information that she can use to determine if he is a good candidate.

We as black women are not taught by our mothers to research a man before allowing him into our lives. Yes, I know that you have done a background check online but I am speaking of the things that go a lot further than the online searches because those don't show the deeply rooted stuff that only being around his parents and friends show.

The old saying is **"birds of a feather flock together,"** is true.

It is your business what this man is doing because if you decide to allow him into your life these things can and will affect you.

If he drinks alcohol, that's in his system and it will affect his sperm cells. Same with illicit drugs, so be warned. Yes, his sperm may be plentiful and he may be fertile but the question is, is his sperm healthy and dis-ease free? And the same goes for the black woman.

We live in an era where the masses think that it is okay for them to put anything into their bodies without causing damage and by the erosion process being so subtle they may not know it until it's too late.

Some people only find out when they have children and the child starts showing signs of dis-ease at an early age.

It is the male that brings in the most damage when it comes to the sperm cells. The child inherits most of the dis-ease and dysfunction from their father. Be it alcoholism, drug addiction, psychosis, or arthritis. There's research that has proven this to be the case.

Now don't get me wrong. Yes, children can receive these things from their mother's when the mother is partaking in such activities, such as recreational drugs and alcohol but when it comes to mental health there is always a male behind it whether it be direct or indirect. It can be directly from the father or it can come from a distant male family member like the grandfather or great grandfather.

Genetics plays a major role in every aspect of our lives. It is never just about you because your genetic makeup involves other parties. These are just some of the events that take place long before procreation and birth.

Then from the moment that we are born into this realm the erosion process has already begun to slightly accelerate. The birthing process alone wears away at the very core of us. From the pressuring and pain of going through the birthing process for the child and the mother, to the detachment of the connected life force of the umbilical cord, and to the attachment if blessed enough, to the breast.

It is this erosion process that slowly causes the psychological and physical scars that are oftentimes unknown to the person that carries them. The process is sometimes so gradual that the person deems themselves not to have any damage at all.

Even in the birthing process both the mother and the child are both in a state of erosion simply because of the birth itself.

The forcing apart of the mother's pelvic bones and the forcing of the child through while the bones are constricted and contorted.

The pain of the birth for both the mother and the child triggers erosion of both the mind and the body that most aren't even aware of and certainly not talked about because the focus is always on a healthy delivery and after the delivery the focus then shifts to going on and all that comes with being a new mother.

Unfortunately, there is no mention of the painful process of what the child has gone through nor of the damage that has been done to the child after birth.

The deeply rooted effects on this child is never addressed because it is deemed as unnecessary. The focus in on the growing process of the body. The development of what society deems as important, from diapers to strollers. Not even aware of the deeply rooted issues that has caused the child to erode.

The psychological damage that never gets addressed slowly turns into an adult that doesn't know how to cope with the everyday issues that arise because as a baby they needed more holding time and sometimes it is the father's preexisting conditions that has been passed along to the child unbeknownst to the mother.

Leaving the mother drained and confused because nothing that she does in an attempt to comfort and soothe the baby works. So, she starts to examine herself thinking that the root of the issue must be in some way her fault. She never stops to examine the father nor does she think about the behavior of her child's father before and during conception as the major cause of her child's dysfunction.

Now this child has become an adolescent and is showing increased signs of dysfunction and now the mother is worried. She now starts to think back at the behavior of the child's father and now it is more apparent that the source of her child's dysfunction is the father.

This is the time that the mother begins to look for solutions and quickly discovers that it is not as easy as she initially thought. Panic may even set in. If her and the father aren't together or communicating she may out of desperation contact him to see if in some way he has a solution to the problem. This step may even be disheartening for her because the father may have changed for the worst and he may still be in his mess. This point of contact may have even made things worse for her and her child.

Now the erosion process has slowly increased again. The child's behavior has taken another turn for the worse while the mother is frantically looking for another way to help her child function in this state.

This is the physical aspects of the dis-ease caused by the erosion process. We have yet to indulge in the spiritual aspects of it.

From early chapter's we know that the spirit plays a major role in our lives. We also know that the spirit needs this body in order to function in this realm and we also know that the body wants to control what the spirit needs. This in itself creates an erosion effect.

Even as children we have learned very early on how to manipulate others to get what we want. Once success at this manipulation process comes in the physical then it is tried with the spiritual, although never successful, it is not for lack of trying and in this attempt at continuously trying to control the spirit the erosion process has increased yet again.

Every time this type of spiritual manipulation is tried sickness and dis-ease are sure to follow because the spirit will not allow you to do such a thing.

As much as the physical you would have you think that you are the master of your own fate in every area of your life, you are not. It is the spiritual you that is the master and when you refuse to adhere to the spirit, erosion is sure to follow.

As you age it is a natural occurrence for the body to deteriorate. You know very well nothing on this planet stays the same. However, it is the things that you do that determines the rate of erosion.

The master key to unlocking your solution and to slow down the erosion process is love. Yes, love. It is the love of self that mends and fixes some of the damage caused by the erosion process.

You must get to a point in your life where you will no longer accept certain things from yourself nor anyone else. There comes a time when you must take a stand against the maltreatment caused by you.

Just as you must accept full responsibility for the erosive behavior in your life because everything leads back to you.

When you love yourself the way that you should, certain things you will never allow.

We all have been at a point in our lives when we are unsure of ourselves but at some point, you must build your self-esteem to a point of worthiness. You must from this moment start to value who you are as a person and as a spirit being.

It is you that will always have you and even with the damage that you have caused to yourself, along with the damage that you inherited, you can still go on to achieve everything that was placed within you, even with the erosion.

You may be broken, chipped, scarred, maimed, and battered but you are not counted out. There is still time. It doesn't matter how long you have been this way. What matters is that you have another chance. There is hope. Some of your damage caused by the erosion process can be fixed. However, it is all up to you. No one else can do it but you.

You must be diligent in your quest to stabilized yourself before you become someone's parent because everything that you are has the potential to become everything that they will become times two.

Now is the time to work on you and that requires you to acknowledge your spirit and learn how to take heed to your spiritual guidance.

« CHAPTER 6 FRACTURES »

It is known that fractures are the cracking or breaking of something and are usually caused by accident or carelessness. Although there are times when fractures are actually done on purpose no matter the cause it can lead to a lifetime of complications if not treated properly.

This works both physically and spiritually.

Most fractures appear to be small in the natural and therefore are overlooked by most. Just because something starts out small doesn't mean that it doesn't have the potential to grow and that growth can be deadly.

For instance, bones are very strong and it takes a great deal of force to cause fractures to your bones. Well the same goes for your spirit.

When you are spiritually grounded things may come that shake you up but they will not break you. It is only through the lack of spiritual awareness that causes the type of negative forces that lead to fractures.

When you neglect your spirit, and do what you want to do in the natural you create the perfect environment for chaos and pandemonium to reign in your physical life.

The cracking of the core of you leaves wounds that have the potential to spiral out of control leaving deeply rooted issues that only Divine intervention can heal.

No one is exempt from the pressures of society and that pressure has the ability to crack your core if you allow it to. It is this pressure that creates a hostile environment for you to live in and if you give into the pressures you are sure to crack.

The spirit is sure to give you settle cues before the fracture is created to allow you ample time to change the behavior that will lead to the fracture.

It is the things that you do and allow that alters the course of your journey and the lack of love that determines how long and painful your detour will be.

An avalanche of trouble will continue to happen to a degree of near death if you are not careful.

You and your ability to cope with what you have done may or may not cripple you for the short term. Each time that you are hurt the pressure to your core intensifies and this pressure creates cracks. These cracks represent mistrust, agony, doubt, betrayal, disappointment, dishonesty, and misuse.

Each time something negative happens it adds another layer to the core of your being. You begin to second guess yourself, leading to more anguish. It is this lack of trust of yourself that also allows others to come in and mistreat you.

You deny the gift within and start to look at everything in the natural instead of in the spiritual. You count on others to comfort you instead of you allowing your spirit to do so.

The outside forces have now become your friends and you no longer listen to the spirit that dwells within. The God in you has been denied the freedom to gently guide you.

You have begun the process of self-medicating trying to soothe the torment that you have caused. Drinking alcohol and using illicit drugs to numb yourself and quiet your correcting spirit.

The demeaning and the devaluing process of yourself is at an all-time high and nothing and no one can stop your downward spiral.

The fractures are causing a tremendous amount of physical and psychological pain. The cracks to your core are not healing at this stage because of your inability to be truthful with yourself.

You walk around pretending that all is well when the pain has almost immobilized you. You smile and laugh with those around you as if nothing is wrong. Putting on airs is what you have become an expert at. Allowing people to see only what you want them to see because you are still good at functioning with your fractures.

The most painful part of this stage is when you come home and night time sets in, this is when you feel the most intense pain, and welcome sleep because it is your way of coping. You feel as if sleep is the magical cure to all that ails you.

Don't get me wrong now, sleep is actually good for you and the body does heal better when you get the proper about of sleep and the spirit also does its best work when you are sleeping. However, with the about of fractures you have you require more than sleep to repair this type of damage.

It takes about 6-8 weeks for a healthy person's body to heal a fractured bone and this also depends on where the bone is in the body. There are several things that come into play when discussing the hue-man body because it is mainly guess work because no two bodies are exactly the same. With that being said just think about how long it would take for multiple fractures to heal on a sick or dis-eased person. Now think about that in terms of the metaphoric fractures that you have received in your mind, body, and spirit from the demonic things that have happen to you during the course of your life.

Every time you step out of the will of God and do what you want to do, even though you know in your heart that it is not right, and will not yield you anything good, you do it anyway and disaster strikes.

There is a penalty for all disobedience and that includes God's children. When you go against what you know is right you must be aware that there is a consequence for this action. The consequence is a crack in your foundation, theoretically that is.

The trauma that you have experienced because of your unwillingness to honor yourself has left behind so many fractures that it will take the rest of this life time to even try to repair some of them.

The underlying cause to these fractures are far deeper than you can ever imagine because the root cause is you and your unwillingness to stop and study yourself and take the necessary steps to change what needs to be changed.

You keep making the excuse that you are doing your best when your best is not enough. When you keep operating in your best mode you are not honoring the spiritual part of you because if you were you would know that the spiritual part of you has the ability to go far beyond what the natural you can do. The spiritual you will always, when set in the leadership role, do what's required.

When you are fighting to stay on course you must at all times be aware that you are first spiritual and second natural and in that order. This knowledge will help you when you get to a point where nothing appears to be working out right. You must learn to stop when things become chaotic because it is a sign that you are off course. It is an alarm from your spirit indicating that you need to be redirected.

There will be moments in your journey when you feel out of touch with the spiritual part of you and this is largely due to the trauma that you have experienced. This trauma has left behind fractures and when some of those fractures healed they left behind internal scars that cause pain and some of this pain is unbearable to say the least.

No one truly knows how deep the damage is because it is multilayered. Some of it is so deep that even a scan of your entire body can't detect it all, from a natural standpoint.

The physical damage coupled with the psychological damage is a good deterrence from the spiritual damage. It is very difficult to stay the course when you have damage to all three layers. That's why it is imperative that you listen to your spirit before this type of damage occurs.

That gut instinct is there for a reason and you must learn to trust your gut instinct because it will never lead you wrong.

If you would be totally honest with yourself, every time you didn't listen to your gut instinct, you in some way or another brought suffering upon yourself. I have told you this before. You must learn to listen to your spirit because when your radar from within starts going off that is your spirit warning you that something is not right. It is always a warning before a fracture. The crack in your core is always a direct result of not listening and adhering to your spirit. I must keep emphasizing this until you get it.

It is not easy to fracture a bone naturally because it requires a great amount of force to do so, just as it is not easy to break mentally because it normally takes several traumatic events to cause a mental breakdown. Now with that you can deduce that it takes an astronomical amount of demonic force to fracture the spirit because the spirit is the core of you. That Holy energy, that never ending life force, that God in you.

All healing requires time and there are of course different stages of the healing process. Nothing and no one completely heals overnight. All fractures require more time to heal than they do to cause and the longer they go untreated the more damage that's likely to be caused.

For instance, when you injure yourself to the extent of a fracture and you keep doing the same type of activity that caused the fracture in the first place, then surely you are to cause more damage than the initial crack and prolong the healing process.

Once the damage is done in the natural the body immediately sends stem cells to start working on the healing even when you aren't aware as to what is happening.

Now in your natural state of unawareness you mistakenly keep trying to function normally with the fracture while the body keeps sending you signals that a crack is present and needs to be attended to, yet you refuse to do what is required to allow the body to heal itself in an expedient manner. The first signal that the body will send to you in the natural is pain.

It's absolutely amazing how many people are walking around on this planet in physical pain, psychological pain, and spiritual pain. Every day is a battle for them as they try to navigate through their day pretending that the pain is not there and the more they try not to acknowledge the pain the worse the pain becomes until it immobilizes them.

Everyone has a different level by which they can handle pain. What one can take the next one may not be able to because we are all different beings with all different capacities.

In these different stages of healing you must keep in mind that in each stage there is a level of pain that you must deal with before the healing comes, if at all.

The first stage of the healing process for some is the most painful because this is the time when the fracture is fresh. The fracture has caused a crack in what was originally produced for you. Now the body must work hard to repair the original back to a more acceptable state because it will never be the same.

This is the reactive stage when the fracture is inflamed and this inflammation is causing the body to react. Without a reaction from the body the stem cells would never be released and the beginning of the healing process will never take place.

When a fracture happens in the natural it's going to start bleeding although the bleeding may not be apparent to you because most fractures aren't apparent to the natural eyes.

The bleeding is a result of the crack in your foundation and at the point of the fracture because of the bleeding a clot will form and then at the end of the fracture that area of bone dies. This death is what causes the inflammation.

Once the body starts sending the stem cells to the fracture your body will now start to repair the damage, this is the second stage of the healing process and in this stage the body will start to lay down a substance called callus and it develops into cartilage, new blood vessels, and finally calcium that eventually turns into bone. Once this is complete now it is time for the body to start its final stage in the healing process.

Stage three of the healing process is now ready to take place and in this stage the fracture is in the restructuring process. The body is using what occurred during stages one and two to make a new portion of bone where the fracture happened. This involves creating a similar bone, connective tissue, and blood vessels. Once this is complete the calloused area that was created during stage two decreases.

These three stages are relevant to the psychological and spiritual process of healing as well. Just with slightly different components.

From a psychological standpoint when the mind has suffered a breakdown it is imperative that you give yourself the proper amount of time to heal. This healing requires you to remove yourself from what caused the break in the first place.

Then after the removal process you will have to start retraining the mind to cope with the traumatic event that caused the break and once this is done then you can move on to acceptance. In the acceptance phase, you will take ownership of everything that has taken place that you contributed to. Here you will also examine how you got to that point and what you need to do to ensure that it never happens again. Once your analyzing phase is over you will start to function in your new mindset and the unhealthy things that you use to do you are no longer done and the unhealthy things that you use to accept you no longer accept.

You have now set a higher standard for yourself because you now know your worth and in this worthiness, you walk in the knowing of who you are and whose you are. This has led you to the point of acceptance of the natural you and acknowledgment of the spiritual you.

The spiritual phase of healing is actually conducive to the healing of the physical and psychological because it is the spirit that is the foundation and the foundation must always be the force by which you are driven.

The spirit will allow certain things to take place in order for you to walk in your purpose, especially when you refuse to adhere to your chosen path.

The reason for you being here on this planet is far greater than the physical aspects of who you are, it is far deeper than the natural you can ever imagine.

Always keep in mind that everything is about cause and effect.

« CHAPTER 7 GASH »

The word gash defined in the natural as a long deep slash, cut, laceration, tear, or wound, depending on its depth can penetrate the underlying tissues, fat, tendon, muscle, or bone. No matter the depth of the gash it will become infected if not properly treated.

A gash is a great metaphoric way of looking at the relationship between the black woman and the black man.

They have been cut so deep that the wound has now become infected because the underlying issues have not been dealt with.

For generations, the black woman and the black man as a whole have been living separate lives from the moment they refused to do what was required of them in the spiritual and with this spiritual disobedience has come a gash so deep that it has penetrated not only the flesh but also the mind and the spirit.

With a gash so wide that neither party can see or feel just how deep the effects are on them. They have deduced that there is no problem. Now with their unwillingness to acknowledge that there is a problem and a major one at that they have hindered the first steps in the healing process.

You are now left with a group of people who are chosen by God, walking around with blinders on pretending that all is well. They're not even willing to take responsibility for the shambles that their lives are in and have the audacity to get angry when someone else doesn't take responsibility for their shambles.

The black woman and the black man are not even mindful of the fact that everyone else is mimicking their behavior. **No one can do to you what you have not already done to yourself.** You will not receive better treatment from anyone else until you start treating yourself better.

Your honor is in treating your own self with respect. Unfortunately, you can't do that until you treat the infected wound caused by the untreated gash that is oozing and gapping, pus filled and painful. Yet you pretend as if nothing is wrong.

So, you create this inflated persona trying to cover up the fact that you are wounded not even realizing that wounded people wound people. You're in pain so you deem it beneficial to cause someone else pain as if it will somehow ease your pain. Where is the logic in that?

You have reduced yourself to a shell of who you were created to be because of your unwillingness to take responsibility for what you have created. For some reason, it is only the things that you deem to be good that you are willing to acknowledge.

Your children are the greatest example of this plight, for those black men who stay this is not for you, and for those that leave you only acknowledge your seed when they grow up and become what you consider to be successful. Then and only then is it daddy's baby.

It's a shame that the infected wound has spread to your children and now they carry the remnants of the gash that you failed to treat. Who wants to be burden with someone else's crap?

In your inability or shall I say unwillingness to acknowledge nor accept who you are you look at yourself as beneath others, inferior even.

The gash is so deep that no one single chosen being can repair it.

This gash was created long before slavery and it was caused by the chosen people, the black woman and the black man caused this gash due to their unwillingness to remain holy. They came to this realm on assignment and during their mission they began to allow the things in this realm to take the place of their creator. They began to replace love with lust and honor with hate.

Nothing satisfied them any longer and seeking the other part of self, became unimportant and irrelevant. They started to see all things as one dimensional and plenty became lord over quality and the oneness of the spirit. This is what opened the gateway and created the gash that is still paramount in 2017.

The world became their home and therefore they abandoned the ambassadorship gifted to them by the Supreme Being. Nothing outside this realm mattered to them any longer. With this breakdown, it became increasingly easier for them to suppress who they truly were and what their purpose for being in this realm was for.

It is imperative that you remove the blinders and see yourself for who you truly are before it's too late. The too late part that I am referring to is your exit from this realm before having achieved your mission.

No matter how many fractures you have there is still hope that the restructured you will be able to complete the task at hand no matter the level of pain that you're experiencing. The pain must not stop you from achieving, use that pain to be your driving force. Allow it to push you into your purpose because there is no purpose without pain.

That pain from those fractured places is a reminder of what you don't need to do again and what you have yet to do. The pain, no matter the severity is a teaching tool, whether seen for the positive or for the negative.

You must over-stand that you have the ability to heal yourself from certain fractures and then there are those fractures that are so severe that you require assistance from someone else to start the healing process.

There comes a point when you have to determine when you need assistance and from which source because there are some things that you will not be able to do alone no matter how gifted and anointed you are.

That initial fracture and all other subsequent fractures have caused a natural and a spiritual imbalance. These imbalances have caused you to malfunction and this has caused you to doubt yourself and your abilities to do what is required to achieve your goals.

It is like a crack in a piece of glass, depending on the nature of the crack it has the ability to stabilize as long as no additional trauma is caused to it but if it is an unstable crack the elements can cause the crack to increase causing further damage to the piece of glass.

Well that is the same way a fracture can be to a bone and metaphorically to the core of who you are as a spirit and natural being. The size of the initial crack is determined by the about of force used to cause the crack in the first place and what happens after the initial fracture is what causes the fracture to increase in size and cause infection.

Where there is a will there is also a way. The decision is yours when it comes to how you want to handle your damage and just because you have broken places doesn't mean that you are damaged beyond repair. The key to your repair is within your willingness to operate within the confines of the inner you. The spirit that dwells within you is the only way to ensure a healthy and safe course of action when it comes to the healing that you seek.

From this moment forward in your healing process make sure you are focused on the outcome and not the problem. See yourself pass the damage.

« CHAPTER 8 HEMORRHAGE »

There is power in the blood, be it inside or outside the body, without blood you can't live. The blood inside your bodily plays a significate role in your vitality. The blood is one of your body fluids and has many functions within the hue-man body. It supplies oxygen to tissues and nutrients to the body.

When the body is functioning properly the blood flow is good and is able to transport and perform its duties without any problems. However, there are times when the body is damaged and causes problems with the blood supply and this causes other problems to occur within the body. Thus, bringing me to the title of this chapter, hemorrhage.

A hemorrhage occurs when a blood vessel ruptures and this rupture causes blood to escape from the blood vessel. A hemorrhage is an excessive about of blood leaking from the blood vessel and if not treated in time can cause death.

Hemorrhages can happen anywhere in the body and there are many causes.

Most blood vessel's burst due to increased pressure in the body. When something is off within the body and causes the pressure in the body to rise to abnormal levels then the body must do something to alleviate the pressure. Just as when you put too much air in a balloon when it only has the capacity for a certain level, the over-abundance will cause the balloon to burst. The same goes for your blood vessels.

Hemorrhages, simply put are caused by too much pressure.

From a spiritual perspective, a hemorrhage is an outpouring of the blood and the blood represents the purest part of the body. The power of the blood for the purpose of healing needs to remain in a certain environment so that its usefulness can be fulfilled.

The blood is so powerful naturally that it can sustain the life of not just the owner of it but even others that it is shared with. It also is a genetic marker. The blood that flows through your body is coded to reveal everything about you physically.

When you allow certain things to enter your body this can cause a malfunction and this malfunction creates pressure and this pressure mounts and builds to the point of eruption. Once eruption happens then of course the blood can no longer continue to be in the area that it was intended to be in so it has to come out.

You have now begun to bleed abnormally and your life is at risk.

On a spiritual prospective the bleed out is from the pressure that you placed yourself under by not doing what was required in the natural to adhere to the spirit. You are bleeding at an alarming rate and require assistance from an outside source to help repair the damage that has been caused by the pressure.

You have become in the world and not of it. You have allowed the natural part of you to create chaos that the spiritual side of you can't tolerate. Now the spiritual side of you has to stop you before further damage is done to your body.

You are hemorrhaging physically, psychologically, and spiritually, simultaneously.

The pressure has mounted to a point of explosion and it is this eruption that has your equilibrium off.

You have become lightheaded with an accelerated heart rate as the blood rushes out the veins whether it is internal or external in the physical sense. This loss of blood has caused the body to work hard trying to repair the damage itself. However, depending on the location, depth, and severity of this damage the body alone may not be able to repair itself without outside assistance.

When the pressure is that of a spiritual matter it is even more deadly because it is coming from a prospective of forces that you aren't about to physically see nor touch. Therefore, this type of repair requires you to rely on the spirit to assist you. This is also where fasting and prayer becomes paramount because this damage is caused by spiritual warfare.

The bleeding that you are experiencing is from the spiritual realm and that of holiness.

You have been spiritually wounded and the power of the blood of holiness is needed. You have bled out to the point where you need a spiritual blood transfusion, along with a spiritual surgical repair.

Your hemorrhaging at an alarming rate because of a self-inflicted wound and this wound requires you to slow down and take a step back in order to analyze every event that led to the bleeding out.

When you decided to take the lead in spite of your spirit warning you to take a step back, you inadvertently took a blow that no hue-man being should have taken. You entered the spiritual battle field when you weren't yet trained to do so.

In your effort to prove that you were ready, you prematurely stepped into an area that was marked off limits. You allowed your flesh to lead instead of your spirit.

You knew you weren't ready but you let others convince you that you were and now that you are hemorrhaging and they see it, the advice is now different. It went from *"you can do it to I wouldn't have done that if I were you."*

You took advice from the outsiders instead of from the insider *(your spirit)*. Fortunately for you all is not lost. You can make a full recovery by removing the negative elements and focusing on your healing.

You can turn the negative aspects of the bleeding out to that of receiving the positive spiritual transfusion. This is where the power of the blood will come into effect.

The spiritual recovery process will work simultaneously with the physical and the psychological.

It is the spirit that has all power because it is of purity and that of holiness. When you abide by spiritual laws injury to yourself is very low.

Yes, there will always be a threat to you in both the spiritual and natural because there are other forces at work. You are and will always be a target because of who and whose you are.

You are gifted and was born to complete an assignment that only you are able to do. No other being on this planet can do what God has assigned you to do and you can't pass the duty off to someone else.

You will along the way encounter some adversity and there will be times when you will bleed out but there is nothing that you can't do within the will of God.

It is within the will of God that you will find rest and in the event of injury be it physical, psychological, or spiritual there is healing.

Within the confines of the will of God you will experience an undeniable love like no other.

A mending and restructuring process that will create a better you. A you that is more in tune with the spiritual you. A you that focuses on the finished product instead of the incompleteness that you feel in this realm.

Once the repairs are made and the bleeding has stopped you will feel anew and revitalized. Your focus will shift again to the mission at hand.

Although scars may be left behind from the injuries that you sustained, you no longer look at them in disgust but rather as a reminder of what you have yet to do and what God has already brought you through.

You have received a fresh anointing and on fire for the Kingdom of God and you are adamant about doing what is required to get where you need to be.

Nothing and no one is more important than you at this point because you have realized that if you do not take care of your body and mind you will not be able to do what your spirit needs you to do. So now taking care of yourself has become a priority.

You are happier and feel more energetic. The things that use to bother you no longer do. You don't feel guilty when you do something for you before you do something for someone else and no has become one of your favorite words.

It is imperative at this stage in the journey that you treat yourself as God treats you. The love and care that God showers you with is an example for you to pattern. You can't keep treating others better than you treat yourself and expect them to mimic you.

You no longer need the bandages that you received when you were bleeding. The hemorrhage has been treated and repaired so stop acting as if the wound is still fresh and open.

You keep covering the injury sight expecting it to bleed out again every time you give yourself permission to love you first.

You are not selfish just because you have learned that you must come first in order to keep going on with the mission.

Your journey requires you to be in the greatest physical and mental shape that you have ever been in so that your spirit can use your body to navigate in this realm to complete this mission.

One of the most profound examples I hear every time I travel by airplane is when the flight attendant starts to give the rules, regulations, and guidelines of the flight and gets to the part when its stated that ***"if the pressure in the cabin drops and the oxygen mask fall, you must put your own oxygen mask on first before you assist someone else with theirs."***

I think about that every time I am contemplating assisting someone before I do for myself.

By the way you don't owe anyone an explanation about why you do for yourself first.

It is your duty to show self-love before you show love to others. You set the standard as a child of God. It is you that show others how to love you by how you love yourself. So, if you start off putting yourself last on your care list then they are going to do the same.

If you are bleeding from a wound are you going to just let yourself bleed without treating the source of the bleeding?

« CHAPTER 9 INCISIONS »

An incision is a precise cut that is done for your betterment. Normally an incision is made in the physical during surgery and a surgical procedure is done to fix something that has malfunctioned on or within your body.

This purposeful cut is typically planned for a specific day and time. During this preparation process, you are given instructions that you must follow to ensure that the surgery goes as planned.

Now, when you look at the process of the precise cutting that must be made in order to repair the damage that was caused you must determine whether the incision is beneficial to you or not.

Once every aspect of the pros and cons have been weighed then you make the decision that best fit your situation.

It is imperative that during this process you keep in mind that some things must be strategically cut from your life for you to succeed.

Not all of the people in your life will be able to complete the journey with you and you must realize this as soon as possible so that you won't waste valuable time.

Time is the most valuable resource you have on this planet and once it's gone you can't get it back, so, you must use it wisely.

Everyone who enters your life enters it for a reason and it is up to you to determine what that reason is because they either come to give or they come to take. It is a rarity that they come to do both. There are also those that come to cause more damage and there are those that come to assist you with your healing process.

I have learned during my journey to place everyone who enters my life into categories. I have two main categories and four sub-categories.

The two main categories consist of:

1. Positive
2. Negative

The four sub-categories consist of:

1. Roots
2. Trunks
3. Branches
4. Leaves

Okay now the main categories are indeed self-explanatory, however the sub-categories require a bit of explaining. I use a metaphoric technique with the sub-categories.

The roots are the people who have been planted in your life from the beginning and they are the ones behind the scenes helping you stand. They are the ones that no one sees but they know that they are there. No matter what happens they remain grounded and rooted in your life.

They assist you in every area of your life and they are strong and resilient. They have a supernatural ability to weather every storm with you. Their supply of support for you is endless because they know that without them you will not be able to complete the journey. You are connected to them both spiritually and physically. They feel what you feel and they have no problems relaying this to you.

They carry the baton when you get tired. They push you to keep going when you feel like giving up and they correct you when you are wrong. They don't want credit for anything that they do. However, they do expect you to do what is required to maintain a healthy balanced relationship with them.

The trunk is the one that stands strong for you and are always seen. They are as vital as the roots will allow them to be because the roots are the key supplier to the trunk. The trunk however, gains its strength from the roots to be there for you.

They are strong resilient people who will take the force of the blows for you if need be and no matter how tough the storm they are there to protect you. You can lean on the trunk and without a shadow of doubt know that they will never let you down. It takes a supernatural force to move the trunk from your life because of the depth of the relationship they have with the roots. As long as you are in harmony with the trunk, obedient to your spirit, and respect the value that the trunk has in your life then rest assured that the trunk is there permanently for you.

The branches are a long-standing support system for you and can withstand a mighty blow before they leave your side. They are the extensions of the truck, placed in your life to be a source of joy, strength, and bliss. The branches may sometimes waver in a storm and depending on the strength of the storm they may break, leaving you when you need them the most, albeit to no fault of their own.

Branches are more susceptible to damage depending on the type of trunk that's in your life because the branches rely heavily on the trunk for support in order to support you.

The branches can sometimes appear to be permanent because of the way they hang around and make you feel. Their intentions are pure and sometimes they may over extend themselves in an effort to support you when in fact they don't have the strength.

The leaves are the ones who come around for a season to provide you with a temporary source of beauty and support. They are bright, vibrant, and colorful. You love being around them and they love being around you. They offer you the little pleasures and spread as much of their beauty around as possible. Their support is short term and seasonal and while they are around they give you their all.

You know that you can't expect anything long term from them and it's not because they don't want to, it's because they just don't have the capacity. They are not created to be permanent and this is something that you must accept.

Your expectations for the leaves must always be that of a temporary agency. It is dangerous to give a temporary person a permanent position in your life because no matter how good they are they are still only a seasonal worker.

Yes, they sometimes come back and if you are blessed with a good seasonal support system if will surely be worth the wait, no matter how many times they leave.

It is those bitter sweet moments that offer some of the greatest rewards. The leaves offer the most profound example of the necessary incisions that you must sometimes allow to heal from other events that have taken place in your life.

The incisions although painful yet necessary and even after the incision has been made there is still a road to recovery that you must follow to ensure that the cutting was effective.

It is painful to remove someone from your life and even when you make a clean precise incision it is still painful and the after effects are more painful than the previous. The decision to cut anyone from your life must be done with the precise intent and the goal should always be for your healing.

You must learn that no matter what you are the key player and everything and everyone in your life comes after you and whomever doesn't over-stand that needs to be cut. You can't keep putting everyone else's healing before your own. You can't keep helping other people and neglecting yourself.

You constantly trying to rationalize why you keep allowing people to be disrespectful and hurtful to you is not acceptable.

You must see things for what they really are, you owe it to yourself. No one gets to sit front and center in your life if you are not front and center in theirs. ***All relationships must be reciprocal.***

Anything one sided is not balanced and a lack of balance leads to destruction for you. Nothing and no one is worth your peace of mind. It should and shall always be about you first.

You must learn to give yourself permission to be you in every area without rationalizing it. You have the right to do what you deem necessary for you without apologizing to anyone.

Happiness is found within you therefore you are the only one that can determine what is best for you.

Your value is not determined by the people in your life nor the things that you possess, it is determined by you knowing your worth and sometimes it takes a while to appraise your value.

The sad reality about the appraisal process is that if you are not careful you will constantly allow those people and things around you to set your value instead of you.

However, the closer you get to knowing the God in you, you will learn that you are priceless and that there is none greater than you.

You are and have always been a one of a kind rare gem and it's your uniqueness that angers the rest because every time they see you they are constantly reminded of the fact that you are the best.

Envy is real and the sooner you realize that the better off you will be because it is this truth that will set you free. The free that I speak of is the free from bondage of other people's opinions.

The only one on this planet that you should be satisfying is you. The satisfaction of you leads to the willingness to be spirit led and when you are spirit led you are walking in truth.

When I speak of satisfaction of self I am speaking of the spiritual self. The part of you that is open to the infinite possibilities of merging all realms in one. Where you are content with the knowledge that all three realms must function accordingly in order for you to do what is required to complete your mission.

It is even in this cutting process that you are able to determine what is necessary to keep or get rid of in order to heal.

Sometimes it is only when the incision has been made that we can see the totality of the damage that has been done and a better determination is then made to remove more.

There are even times when the incision is made and you realized that you have to make multiple cuts to ensure that all of the infected part has been remove so that healing can be done affectively.

The cutting away of people that you deem vital can be very disheartening especially when you rely on them more than you do on yourself.

No one in your life that's not doing their part can remain in because everyone has a role to play and it's not fair to you to allow such behavior.

The price of them remaining in your life is too high. You have not gotten a return on your investment. They have even become a liability to you instead of an asset and liabilities aren't acceptable.

You give and give and give and they take and take and take. ***Aren't you tired of this foolishness?***

Removing what is harmful is essential to your healing and the sooner you do so the healthier you'll become. Yes, you will be left with scars and no you will never be the same however the scars left behind from the necessary incisions are a constant reminder that it was to save yourself from any further damage and the changed you is better than the old you. You are now better equipped to take the next steps in your journey without the excess baggage placed on you by others who refused to carry their load.

There will be times when the scars from the incision will still cause you a great deal of pain when you focus on the negative aspects of why you had to make the incisions in the first place and it is normal to do so but you must also remind yourself when those moments come of the fact that without taking the initiative you would not be where you are now in your journey.

Those that were cut out of your life no longer had your best interest at heart and this caused them to no longer have relevance in your life. Everyone in your life has a role to play and every role must be of a positive aspect because the negative is already taken by the outsiders. No insider should ever be allowed to play both roles because this is deadly to you.

Unfortunately, there are those times where your team mates will appear to be all for you when in fact they have ulterior motives. You must at all times be aware of those who play both sides.

These are the ones who show signs of envy and often than not low key say doubtful and hurtful things then turn around and say, "I'm sorry I didn't mean any harm." Sure, they did.

Your team should consist of those that are for you and not against you. When there is someone always throwing shade that is not and I repeat not your ally.

Your team mates are an extension of you and they are to be supportive and encouraging. They correct you when you are wrong and praise you when you are right. They bring out the best in you.

Over-standing the roles that each person in your life plays and knowing when to make the necessary cuts is paramount to the success of your mission while on this planet.

There may even come a time when key players have to be cut when your life is in jeopardy. You must at all times be aware that nothing and no one outside of you is more important than you.

Let's look at the tree again. There are some circumstances that require the tree to not only loose leaves but also branches to save the other parts of the tree and depending on how much damage the tree has it may have to be cut at the trunk.

This is why it is important to pay attention to the early signs of negativity coming from your team before it destroys every area of your support system, including the roots.

« CHAPTER 10 JAGGED »

Jagged is the rough and uneven cuts inflicted upon you and more often than not for the intent to save you. These jagged cuts are typically made without any preplanning and in emergency situations.

It is when you are facing an immediate crisis that these jagged cuts must be made. There is no time for precision at this point. It is a life or death type of situation where there is no need for pleasantries.

At this stage in the process being nice is not required because you have been placed in a situation where it is do or die. No more chances can be given.

You have said and done the same things over and over again and to no avail they still refuse to adhere.

You have questioned yourself repeatedly about why, when, and how did you get to this point? And the answers are always the same. You didn't do what was required! You kept making excuses for the shortcomings of others and took the blame every time they decided to mess up. They refused to take responsibility for their wrongs and you failed to allow them.

Thinking you can fix everyone and save everybody when it is not your assignment. You were assigned to be of assistance, to help! But when they saw how good you are they decided to play on your intelligence and kind heart and coerce you into doing all the work for them.

Once you completed the work for them they saw you as a threat and no longer useful because they didn't want anyone else to find out that it was in fact you who did all the work and not them.

They wanted the glory and all the credit but what they failed to realize was that they still needed you because your work will never be complete because the system always requires annual upgrades that they aren't equipped to handle because they do not know how the program was set up in the first place.

Now it is time for the annual upgrade, the previous work is no longer valid and the people they have fooled into thinking that they completed the work alone wants to see more and unfortunately for them, they can't deliver.

When they realize that they have in fact played themselves far more than they have played you now they want to run back to play the I'm sorry and I need you card. When really, they aren't sorry for you only for themselves and yes, they do need you and always have but in their mind, it was only temporary.

People like this never want to learn how to do things on their own. They are always looking for someone else to do it for them and in their quest to better themselves by misusing you, you end up short changed.

Every relationship you enter no matter the person should always be positive. The good must always outweigh the bad. You are to be the compliment of one another.

The scars left behind from the jagged cuts you have had to make and receive where not essentially necessary but they did happen and there is good that can and will come from it.

There are moments when you must feel the pain from these unexpected wounds so that you will also see the value in receiving them.

The lessons are far more powerful than the tragedy.

It is imperative that you examine every aspect of the events as they unfold in your life because there is meaning behind all of them.

The rough nature of this type of cutting leaves you with unsightly scars that may not ever completely heal however you must learn how to function with the unhealed scars.

When you develop a positive attitude towards the scars that you possess you will start to see the value in having them.

It is the holding onto the values set by society that keeps you bound in the unrealistic expectations of others.

Your mindset towards yourself is what will make or break you. Your journey is dependent on how you value who you are and what your reason for being is.

The unfortunate aspects of the roughness and mistreatment that you have had to endure from yourself and others have left you doubtful and resentful towards both yourself and others.

The power of disappointment can have a lasting negative impact on the way you view yourself and others.

The painful but necessary cutting has caused you to constantly be on alert and cautious of everything and with good reason. The unfortunate part of this state is that you have started doubting your instincts and the second guessing has delayed your progress.

The removal of certain people albeit necessary has left you with unsightly scars because of their rough mistreatment of you. These scars have penetrated all three layers of who you are as a being and because of this you have isolated yourself in an effort to protect yourself from any further harm.

Those that try to get close to you don't know why you are the way that you are and you have not felt the need to explain because you know they wouldn't over-stand.

Your inability to fit in is a clear indication that you are not supposed to. Those that are set apart suffer from the apparent wounds of those that envy their God given gifts.

You must realize that your path at times will be a lonely and misunderstood one and no matter what you've done there will be moments when the scars will hurt.

As you move further along in your quest your level of pain will increase and those scars you thought had healed will seem fresh.

You have been ripped repeatedly by those that you trusted and held dear to your heart and just when you thought that all was well you let someone else near and they disappointed you and you had to cut them abruptly from your life in a last-ditch effort to protect yourself. It is this repeated cycle that has you in panic mode and this has wounded you even more.

The reality of what you are going through isn't just a physical issue, nor is it just psychological either, it is also spiritual. This makes it harder to pinpoint the exact course of treatment, especially since you keep trying to treat a spiritual wound physically and a psychological wound physically. Each wound requires its own course of treatment and there are times when those treatments must be done simultaneously.

Those jagged wounds have been left behind by your so-called friends who stabbed you in the back with betrayal. The spouse who lied and cheated. The dearest children you gave birth to that disrespected and embarrassed you privately and publicly.

However, the deepest and unsightliest wound was the one that you caused yourself. You hurt you more than anyone else could have. You ripped a gaping hole in the core of you and now you are struggling to repair it. As you try and try to repair the jagged edges they just aren't fitting together the way you thought they would.

You have worked tirelessly to pull everything back together as they were before but you have not realized that the jagged edges will never mend back together as they were before.

The edges have thickened making it difficult to merge in the physical and psychologically to trust yourself and spiritually to adhere.

All hope is not lost. No matter the reason or severity of the wounds you can still function with them.

« CHAPTER 11 KELOIDS »

Stop waiting on someone else to come and save you. You have the ability to do that yourself. You keep waiting on a man-made God instead of relying on the God made God that resides inside of you. You keep hoping and praying for someone else to come along and do what you know you need to do for yourself.

You keep checking on the latest freedom march so that you can attend but when it comes to self-examination you cringe.

Why is it that you would rather believe in the sugar coated lies to be fact but the facts you deem to be sugar coated lies?

The truth that you seek is and has always been within you and you know it. It's just that once you acknowledge the truth that you are in possession of, you will be held accountable for knowing it, so you pretend that you aren't aware thinking that this pretense will keep you safe from the accountability that's attached with that truth.

Since you entered into this realm you have neglected your duties and chose to bask in the falsities of this world.

You have for centuries pretended as if you are direct descendants of this era, when clearly you know that you aren't. You are very well aware that this realm is not your permanent home yet you are doing everything within your power to make it so.

Denying the truth doesn't make it any less true just as embracing a lie doesn't make it any less of a lie.

You can choose to do whatever you want to do because it is your choice but there is a consequence to that action. The unfortunate part to this is that you will not be the only one to bear the burden. Your direct descendants will more than likely suffer as well for the deeds that you have done.

The consequences of your actions will leave a lasting imprint in the fabric of your lineage. You keep waiting and wasting valuable time hoping that someone other than you will come along and do what you were created to do.

You know the work that's required will take you away from the pretense and at this point and time pretending feels good to you.

The fake persona is the key to your fake happiness because real is too much for you.

So, you walk around with the scars covered up and some even repaired to look more attractive hoping that no one will notice the damage that you have caused.

The scars whether notice by others or not are still there and because of some of the things you have done some of the scars have increase in size and has caused more damage. You have caused what was supposed to be a small thin line to stretch and thicken into a keloid.

What should have been a minor scar has escalated into a big one because you did not follow the directions given to you.

Some of you have developed keloids because you weren't given any directions and was left to treat yourself. It was then that your mistreatment of the wound caused the developing scar to take a turn for the worse.

You weren't told to rest, relax and not put unnecessary pressure on the wound. So, you unknowingly did what you thought was best and your best messed you up because your best was not what was required.

You have been trapped in a maze due to the fact that you thought you doing your best was a good thing. Not even realizing that it was something far greater than your best. You have been trained to function in one dimension, focusing only on what you can see and feel. You have suppressed the spiritual aspects of who you are and why you are here.

You have taken on the religion of the others and adopted it as your own, while denying the spirit of holiness that dwells within you. This denial has caused a ripple effect that has thrown everything off for you.

It has allowed the others to tell you how to feel, what to do, and how to think. It is as if you have become a robot, controlled by the remote of the others.

You have stopped thinking for yourself and doing for yourself. You have developed this they owe me and are going to treat me better someday, while still singing "we shall overcome."

The only way for the chosen people to overcome is by the chosen people to get off of their derrieres and do what is required.

You have waited and waited and waited for what?

How many generations have suffered while you waited?

How many more generations will suffer before you wake up?

How much more damage will you allow?

How many scars do you have to develop before you realized that the current method is not working?

When will you pick up the blue print and use it?

When will you stop denying who and whose you are?

When will you stop making excuses?

When will you do what's required?

You have developed a keloid because of the overgrowth of scar tissue. Your wound in essence has created another wound to repair and protect the initial wound. You have a wound on top of a wound that appears to have healed when in actuality it has not.

The coverup has made things worse and at this point you have been looking for alternative methods to assist with the repairs. You want it to be better so you keep trying new things hoping that each one is the one and it is not.

There will come a time when you must accept the fact that the scar is there and you must learn to live with it if you are not willing to do what is required to change it. Just know that even with the changing of the scar it is not an indicator that it will be back to its original state.

This is for all areas of your life that have left you scarred. You will never be the same, this is a fact. However, you can make the choice to accept the changed you and give yourself permission to let the changed you forge ahead.

Being scarred doesn't mean that you are damaged to the point of no use. It is because of the scars that you are more valuable when you are productive. In this state of productivity, you must learn to bask in the positive aspects of who you are no matter the circumstances. So, what, you didn't get to the point when you wanted to but you still got there. Yes, it was detours along the way because of your refusal to listen and adhere to your spirit. You want so badly to be only hue-man that you denounce and deny the spirit that dwells within you. Stop thinking that if you just keep pretending that you don't hear it or feel it, it will just magically disappear. Your denial is only prolonging the inevitable.

You use your multilayered scars as an excuse to prolong the work that is required to get you where you need to be and every time you get to the door marked breakthrough you cringe and turn away. You keep saying that you want it but you really don't because if you did you would take the necessary steps to get to where you need to be and kick that door open.

Your work on you requires time and multiple steps to peel back all the layers of damage you have caused to yourself before you can even fathom dealing with the damages that you have allowed to be done to you by others.

Some of these steps will take years to complete and you must be ready to deal with all that comes with the healing process because sometimes healing is just accepting what is and letting go of what isn't.

Just because you didn't get what you thought you needed or wanted doesn't mean that it wasn't meant to be yours. There are times when the people that are on the other end of the spectrum simply didn't do their part.

Yes, when there are more than one party to any facet of your life, you can be let down, disappointed, and outright cheated out of your blessings. When you are waiting on someone else to do their part and they refuse there is nothing you can do except find another way, move on and find another person. Don't keep wasting valuable time on a person who has no intentions of doing what is required when it comes to you.

Stop praying for something that you know for a fact will never be what you want nor need it to be in that individual because they're not equipped to be it.

There comes a time when you must accept that your time with that person has run its course and it's okay. You needn't waste any more time nor energy on a person who refuses or just can't be what you require.

You have to decide what's more beneficial for you and clinging to a person more damaged than you that refuses to deal with their damage is not healthy for you.

The scars left behind from your own wounds require your immediate attention. You can't fix anyone else's wounds so you might as well get to working on your own.

You must learn when to let go of what doesn't work for you and focus on what does. It's okay to want more and it's also okay to want less. Yes, I said less! There are times in your life when you have overextended yourself to the point of regret. You have worked so hard at over achieving thinking that it would bring you the ultimate satisfaction and happiness when in fact it did the very opposite. Now you have all these things and a boat load of misery to go with it because you thought these things would repair all of the broken places and it didn't.

Now the keloid has stretched even wider and the pain has returned. Now you go looking for a quick way to relieve it and the relief doesn't last as long as you had hoped. You seek outside help and to no avail it doesn't take away the pain either. It just eases up a bit for a short time then returns with a vengeance. So now you decide to try more alternative routes and go deeper into self-medicating but now with illicit drugs, illicit sex, and alcohol. You will try anything now to take the pain away but nothing so far has worked and now even the edge off is not working either.

You have even contemplated suicide because the slow death is taking too long. You do not over-stand why is it so difficult to be at peace and achieve the happiness that you need. Not knowing that the peace and happiness are already within you and it is your scars that are stopping you from feeling the peace and the happiness.

Everything you want and need all starts from within but you keep searching without.

« CHAPTER 12 LESIONS »

The black man. The mightiest of all men. The most feared, the most hated, and the most scarred among all men on this planet.

The lesions that the black man carry have been passed down from one generation to the next and there has been this misconception that everything bad has been gifted to the black community by the black woman.

Upon further analysis, you can deduce that this damage is so deeply rooted that the responsibility of its source has to be share and in sharing the greatest blame must fall on the black man.

The black man has been labeled as the epidemy of failure because of his lack of unity within the family structure.

When you look at the black family as a whole the majority of the homes are ran by single black females because of the non-existence of the black male.

The black man has left his offspring and chose not to look back. As a result, you have black babies growing up without their black fathers.

The black woman then tries to over compensate for the lack of the black man in the household by trying to play both roles. It is in this duel role playing that she quickly learns that she is failing miserably but pretends that all is well.

Deep down the black woman knows that she can't handle this task alone but also knows that she has no other options because the black man that she held near and dear to her heart has left her. So, she does what she knows how and that's survive. However, there is not one moment that goes by where she isn't hoping, wishing, and praying that her black man will return to be the head, the husband, the father, the protector, and the provider.

The hours have become days, the days have become weeks, the weeks have become months, and the months have become years and still she is hoping and praying for the same.

The black woman knows that she has been let down so she hopes and prays that just maybe her black man would at least come back for his off spring and even that he doesn't do.

The black man has moved on and started creating another family and pretends that the first one doesn't exist because it had to be her that failed and not him. She was the one that couldn't keep her man. She was the reason why he couldn't stay. It was that black woman. It's always that black woman.

The black man has this hatred for the black woman that gave birth to him because in his mind she is the one who failed to maintain a proper relationship with his father and made him grow up without him.

Everyday this child was fed and nurtured by a mother who did what she knew how to do and that's survive. She wanted her black man but her black man didn't want her.

She lied for her black man to his offspring. She told them that daddy went away for a short time and he will be back but after those days turned to months and those months turned to years she had to come up with another lie for her black man. She didn't want her children to know that their father didn't want them because he didn't want her. She didn't want them to know that they were casualties of her war. Her war to keep the black man and be different than her mother and her mother's mother.

But how could she have been any different when the black man wasn't any different than his father or his father's father?

They, the black woman and the black man didn't even realize that they had been given a gift from their parents and the gift was a bag filled with strongholds.

Here it is these highly anointed gifted spiritual beings can't get it together. They can't seem to figure out why they keep doing the same things as the generation before them when clearly, they are smarter. No pun intended.

They vowed to be better, to make it work no matter how. But it didn't work and no matter how never happened because the lesions where to many.

They both carried scars that hadn't been treated properly and they both needed time to heal unfortunately neither knew it.

They thought that what they felt for one another was enough to weather any storm unfortunately it wasn't even the storms that caused the breakup, it was the lack of knowing how to cope within a unit with the preexisting damage.

They entered into this union with preconceived notions that once they were together all would magically be perfect and whatever damage caused from the past trauma would magically disappear. When in all actuality it magnified and intensified it. Now you have two people trying to join as one crippled by the dual severity of one another's pain.

They have join their bodies for a brief moment during their sexual act and this has caused even a greater degree of trauma because neither one of them was truthful about why they wanted to have sex in the first place. Each person came with their own hidden agendas. It is unfortunate that each not only had their own hidden agenda but also their hidden fears of what would happen if they told the truth about what they really wanted, so they deem it necessary to hide the truth to get what they wanted.

The black man has made a mockery of the union with the black woman and has not even given it a second thought. This same black man has the nerve to body shame, belittle, and demean the black woman.

The black man in all his shame still holds a vital link to the repairing process of the black family. He must embark on this quest to find the true meaning of who he is and why he is here. He must stop making excuses as to why he has not upheld his part of the spiritual agreement.

There comes a moment where the black man has to come face to face with the lack of full responsibility on his part in the demise of the black family. In all of his vacancies he has chosen to continuously blame the black woman for his lack in all areas.

The black man has refused to acknowledge the fact that he is a God and has taken on the persona as a peasant in this land.

The black man and the black woman are sleeping on the fact that they are the true chosen ones and that there is no savior coming to rescue them. They are in fact the rescuers. It is up to the chosen ones to do what is required to bring about the change that they seek. It is in fact their duties to do so.

In their quest to be better humans they have forgotten that they are **HUE-MANS**. The children of the **SUN**. They have not begun to tap into who they are because of their inability to adhere to the spirit part of self. They truly think that this is it, this realm that is. They are afraid to silence themselves long enough to hear their spirit direct them to the right path.

The black man and the black woman have been so distracted by the things of his world that they have blatantly chosen to walk around with blinders on.

In their pretense, they keep doing the same things over and over again expecting to yield different results.

In this mass extermination process they have brought upon themselves the destruction of not just them but their offspring. It is only when someone else exterminates one of them that they recognize that what they have been doing is not the proper way towards true salvation. You keep saying that you are seeking salvation without even knowing what the meaning of salvation is. Then you have the audacity to say you want deliverance and I say, "deliverance from what?" The meaning of salvation is preservation or deliverance from harm, ruin, or loss.

If you claim you are saved you do not need deliverance nor the salvation that you constantly seek. You keep going on and on and praying over and over for what you already have. There is no need when you already have it in your possession.

You have been tricked into thinking that the others have what you need when in fact they do not. You are the only one in possession of what you need.

I am in awe every time I see the lack of unity the black people that have been chosen by The Most High God to rule and reign over everything in this world have. The black women and the black man have been created to be present in this space and time to rule as God instructed.

The many lesions that cover you physically, psychologically, and spiritually has delayed your awakening. You carry a burden that wasn't yours to carry because of the choices that your ancestors made without regard for what would happen in the future. Now you are here paying for what the ones in the past have done, coupled with what you have done in the present. The past has affected your present and left uncertainty for the future.

However, there is still time because you are still here. You must awaken from the sleep that you are in and totally connect with your spirit before it's too late.

The reconnecting of the black woman and the black man must be done to ensure that this course of destruction is changed.

It is this hope and trust that you put in the others that you need to take back and put in yourselves.

You have been trained to think that what they have is better but if you would just open your eyes you will see that they have always wanted what you have. You have always been better even in your state of lack. You have always had more spiritually. You have always been the one with the intelligence that supersedes every other species.

You gave away what was not yours to give. God equipped you with the ability to see signs and wonders yet you allow others to trick you into thinking that it was bad. You then looked at your God given treasures as a curse and became resentful towards them. So, every time the black man looks at the black woman he is reminded of what he has yet to do. He is reminded of his refusal to comply with his spirit. He is reminded of his failures in the natural and in the spiritual. The black man subconsciously resents the black woman for being a mirror that shows his imperfections so he runs from her as soon as he feels her spiritual power.

As long as the black woman is operating only in the natural the black man is tolerant of her but as soon as she starts to awaken to her spiritual voice then the conflicts increase.

The black woman has been blamed for the downfall of the black man ever since man made religion. It is senseless to try to annihilate the black woman simply because you are afraid of her spiritual awakening.

The black man in his simple mindedness has refused to accept the black woman for who she is. She is his birther. She incubated him. She nurtured him inside and outside of her womb. She fed him from her breast with the milk of the God's yet she is hated by him that she bore.

The black man has on every facet tried to erase the black woman from all things physical and spiritual. To the point of always referring to God as only Father and even excluding her from the Holy trinity. Yet in all of this she is still the one to give birth to him.

The black woman is told that she has no power when she is actually all power. Whatever the black man has given her she has multiplied, increased, and added to. Even in his disrespect towards her, she is still the first one to run onto the battle field for him. This same black woman who was left to fend for herself. She still weeps at night and yearns for the black God on earth that she was granted that refused to accept his spiritual position.

This black woman in her quest to keep what's hers is called bitter, angry, loud, rude, and unworthy when she demands what is owed to her.

The black man not knowing that once he taps into his spiritual self that he becomes a magnet to both negative and positive and that the others can see his awakening starting and wants to at all costs stop it from happening.

The awakening process in its early stages leaves the black man groggy and disoriented. In this state, it is easy for him to be misled by the others.

It is at this point that the black woman guides him to his purpose only for him to see it as misguidance. Both are now frustrated with one another. The black woman because she is in a more advanced state of the spiritual awakening and the black man for the same reason.

Deep down the black man knows that the black woman has the advantage and this terrifies him. The more advanced she is the more threaten he feels.

The black man at this stage is outwardly manly but inwardly boyish. He appears to have grown into adulthood because of his outwardly body size and stature but inwardly he is still that scared little boy who needs the reassurance of his mother.

This fact the black man doesn't want the black woman to know for fear of being portrayed as weak and timid.

The black man for generations has suppressed the little boy inside of him who wants and very much needs to be nurtured without criticism. He wants and needs to be able to lay in the black woman's lap and be free from the pains of this world. He wants and needs to be at peace in his vulnerability with the black woman without recourse. The black man wants and needs to be handled within the confines of his bedroom by the black woman like the God that he is even when consciously he isn't aware.

The black man unaware of the God that he is suffers from dis-ease and contempt. He struggles with his identity both naturally with his conscious and spiritually with his subconscious.

In his quest to validate himself he misuses people and things as a way to somehow feel better about himself even to the point of overcompensating with fancy cars, clothes, and money. To him these things have become his God since he doesn't know that he is in fact a God himself so he settles for the quest to be called king by who he deems to be a peasant. He purposely searches for someone who he deems to be beneath him so that he may feel superior. This gives him a quick fix from the lesions that he suffers from.

Perception is the key to unlocking your door to healing because the way you perceive things dictates how you handle them, so when you change your perception you change the wound.

« CHAPTER 13 MAIMED»

The black woman in her quest to heal the black man has been maimed by him. The damage is so extensive that it can't be repaired. The spirit is very well aware of the damage that was caused to the flesh because the spirit was affected by the damage as well.

You are a spirit being having a hue-man experience. The thought of that alone is permanently damaging. I often think of the trauma that the spirit must endure trying to get the flesh to comply. It must be very disheartening when you (the spirit) knows what to do but is hinder from doing so because the armor (the flesh) you're in is malfunctioning.

This body suit that houses the spirit is susceptible to damages that the spirit directly is not. However, it is the indirect hits that the spirit takes that causes trauma throughout all the realms. The physical body is required so that the spirit can function in this realm. The spirit without this body can't be seen nor heard by everyone that's unawakened. The task that the spirit needs to complete must be done within the confines of the body. What makes it difficult is that the body wants to do the direct opposite of what the spirit needs.

This realm is a controversial one where fleshly things look more appealing than things of the spirit. It is the desire for what can be physically seen and touched that has cause a proverbial crack in the core of the body and this crack has left the body vulnerable to permanent damage. Although permanently damaged, all is not lost because even with this type of extensive damage you can still function with it.

You will have to learn alternative methods of coping and yes it may take a little longer to complete the task but you can still complete it. These set backs are only there because of your unwillingness to comply with your spirit.

The spirit will teach the body how to function with the alternative methods because the spirits desire to do what is required is stronger than the bodies desire to give up.

Even in those moments of doubt and despair the body can still hear the spirit although it may not want to. That inner voice is so powerful that it will not be silenced no matter what the circumstance.

This is one of the reasons why we have so many people self-medicating. They are trying to silence the spirit within. Their need to be drunk or high to numb and silence what's within drives them to do foolish and deadly things. This need is stronger than anything else physical to them. No matter how, they will find a way to continue this silencing process of the spirit, although ineffective.

There are two processes of silence. One is to hear the spirit and the other is to not hear the spirit. When you embark on a spiritual journey to purposely silence the body long enough to hear clear concise directions from the spirit then that is always a positive thing.

However, when you purposefully embark on an alcohol and drug binge to silence the spirit within you are surely headed on the road of destruction. This behavior will always lead you in the direction of negativity. Illicit drugs and alcohol are demonic gateways. They only temporarily numb you and once it wears off you actually feel worse than you did before you took the substance.

There is no sure way to get around dealing with the permanent damages that were caused by other's nor by you. There will come a time when you must come face to face with the events that lead to the trauma that caused the damage, that caused the scars. Nothing and no one can stop this from happening and when it does happen it will either make you stronger or kill you literarily.

Some of you would even welcome a quick instantaneous death because the pain from the trauma is too much to bear at times. The death that you seek unfortunately will not come fast enough for you because your mission on this planet is far greater than the trauma that you have experienced and you can't leave until it is completed. You are only delaying the inevitable by doing what you know will not yield you anything positive. You aren't always operating in a state of unawareness. There are clearly moments when you know exactly what you are doing and why.

In your quest to do what you want you have become a master at deception and this has unfortunately for your victims allowed you to get away with things that normally you wouldn't be able too.

You have learned in your maimed stated to maim others. You have adopted this tit for tat mentality. They did it to you so you must now do it back to them, even if the them are not directly involved in your maiming process.

Your damages have far superseded the body, it has directly affected the mind as well. You no longer rationalize like you use to. There are no boundaries set for you any longer. No limits as to what you won't do that yields the negative results that you seek. You have developed a desire for all things negative and put away the desire for anything positive. You have waged war against yourself and there is nothing anyone can do for you, unless it coincides with the destructive path that you have chosen.

Your drive to do that which is negative has become lord of your life and you make no apologies for it either. Even in your shame you continue to lie to yourself, as if no one else knows. You even pretend like you are not bothered by the glares and the stares from those around you, when in all actuality it is tearing you apart. You don't like the fact that other people can see your damage and it bothers you even more when they see the damage that you caused to yourself because that damage you can't rationalize as easily as the damages caused by someone else.

You in all of your destructiveness still want to be better but you know that better requires a different state of mind. You know that the negative behavior must stop. You also know that the work required to obtain the positive is not going to be easy. The things that you have allowed to happen in your life because of your naiveté burns you like lava especially now that you know better, unfortunately for you, hindsight will not change the events.

The pain felt because of the trauma has you paralyzed in key areas of your life and because of this paralysis you can't function in what is deemed to be the normal way. Albeit true there are still ways to navigate through this terrain called life. You can still get to where you need to be by using the alternative methods. You have been taught to do what is required no matter the circumstances, so do it.

It's okay to cry out in pain, it's okay to weep, it's okay to feel like giving up. It's okay. You have a right to feel whatever it is that you need to feel to get pass this moment of hurt. All of this is part of the healing process. You must fight to get where you need to be and in this fighting process you must also keep in mind that you will never be the same and that too is okay.

Even with the loss that you have encountered you are still more valuable than those around you and even in your state of loss you have still won something and that something is a more valuable, graceful, loving you.

It took you to have something taken away so that you could see the real value in who you truly are. Sometimes it's the things that you hold onto that has the greatest ability to cause the greatest harm and then there are times when the letting go brings about the greatest reward.

As you walk the rest of your journey in this state of maim always remember that in your brokenness you are still more whole than you ever were before. The state of wholeness is not contingent on all of your body parts being intact, it is contingent on your spirit being able to lead.

« CHAPTER 14 NICKS »

Free will is one of the greatest gifts that the Divine Creator gifted to you and with free will comes a greater responsibility. You can do whatever you want just keep in mind that there is a consequence to any and all choices that you make. Some of the choices may cause you to nick yourself in the process. These nicks no matter how small can and will still cause pain and may even leave behind some scars.

Nicks may seem insignificant initially because of the size, due to this fact, you may deem it unnecessary to treat them.

You waste so much time on mundane things not realizing that every day you wake up you're one-day closer to death. You're so focused on the pain that you have refused to bask in the moment of purpose. Your time as valuable as it is, is still short. Love yourself enough to stop and cherish the time that you do have. Relish in the things that bring you joy, peace, and happiness. Balance yourself by giving yourself permission to feel more positive because you have had more than your share of negative. ***"Life itself is but a vapor that soon pass away."*** When you take that into account it makes all the negative stuff seem so trivial.

I am in no way trying to minimize your pain nor am I trying to give you a reason to give up. I want to bring better clarity to your life by showing you just how glorious you are when you walk in your truth no matter how painful.

These nicks that you have aren't stopping you from doing what is necessary. It is the nick in time that is more important than all of the scars that you carry.

The moments when you laugh out loud just because you can and those moments when the pain feels more like purpose.

You have no need to hurry death because death is a certainty for you. So, I implore you to live, I mean truly live. You have so much to accomplish while you are still here. This is the time for you to leave your foot prints in the sand and your blue print to your legacy.

The things that happened to you shouldn't be allowed to hinder you from your purpose but to guide you to it. If you would only just change the way you view your tragedies, you will see that each and every one of them pushed you to do what was required to get you one step closer to fulfilling your purpose on this planet.

Yes, some of the tragedies could have been avoided. Yes, you wish things were different. Yes, you have regrets. Yes, it is okay to feel this way. Learn to allow yourself time to experience life from your spirits perspective. Give yourself permission to be unapologetically you, flaws and all by embracing all things you.

Don't worry about what other's will say because you must live your life according to your purpose. No matter what choices you make, you will be the one to reap the benefits or bare the burdens.

No matter how small the wound it's still a wound nonetheless and must be treated as such. Like for instance you nick your finger with a pin, it's still going to hurt, ask a diabetic.

Nicks are pricks, small in nature but all the more painful. The size of the trauma is not a clear indicator as to the amount of pain that you will endure.

If you have to ask a person, "can I trust you?" There is no need to do so because you already know the answer. Trust just like Love doesn't need to be asked for because it is freely given.

All pain once felt in its entirety can also be a great release, just as a pregnant woman right after birth. It is at that moment right before delivery that she must endure the greatest pain in order to give birth to her promise.

There is purpose in your pain if you will allow yourself time after the trauma to see it. When you get to a point in your life where the pain that you're feeling is so intense that you feel like you're literarily choking from it, that's when you will know that you are about to receive the fullness thereof. The promise, the purpose, the delivery.

You are the keeper of your treatment, the provider of your healing, the source of your awakening. It is and has always been up to you.

You do not have to keep allowing pain to be the driving force in your life because you are worthy of life after the pain, if you want it.

Whatever you want you can have, if you are willing to do what is required. You keep falling short because you have been trained to think that doing your best is all that's needed but contrary to what you have been taught, it is not. What is needed is for you to dig deep within and do what's required to bring about the results that's needed.

I will use the diabetic as an example again. A diabetic depending on the severity of the illness may be required to stick their finger 3 to 4 times a day to monitor the blood glucose levels. Every time they prick their finger it hurts and they never get use to the pain. They must keep track of the blood sugar levels by pricking the fingers. As painful as it is they must do it because it is what's required so that the doctor will know if the treatment is working or if the dose needs to be changed. No matter how often or how long it takes in order to manage their illness this is a part of the process. No, they don't want to, but the pain is part of getting to the promise.

Inflicting the pain upon themselves so they can get an accurate view of their blood sugar levels so they can determine if their food intake is either helping the illness or making it worse dependent on the type of diabetic they are. The course of this action ensures that the diabetic knows what they are dealing with in terms of their blood glucose levels.

The point that I am driving at is that sometimes the things that we are going through are necessary, the pain is necessary for the long-term betterment of our lives. Some trauma is inherited, some inflicted by other's, and some self-imposed.

There are moments in your life when you must bear the nicks in the short-term so that you can benefit from them in the long-term.

Sometimes when the root cause of your pain appears to be small it is of something far greater. The pain no matter the source must be examined. The search is always for the root cause even if self-inflicted you must know why?

No pain no matter how small is significant.

You are the only one who can determine the severity of your pain although someone else may be able to help you determine the reason.

Nicks can also come in time to save you from something worse. Those small pricks no matter how painful can save you from an even greater pain or even loss of life.

The process of discovery is vital to the development of self-assurance and awareness. You the greatest gift to you, must learn to value every moment that you have even in the mist of the pain that you deal with daily. No one and I mean no one is void of some type of pain be it physical, psychological, or spiritual. It's just that some are aware and others are not.

« CHAPTER 15 OPPROBRIUM »

The word opprobrium has many meanings and the one that best fits this chapter is harsh criticism.

Some of the greatest pains experienced by you was from the mouth of someone closest to you. The tongue is as sharp as a two-edge sword when use in a negative manner.

There is no one on this planet that is old enough to speak that hasn't said something negative before be it to someone else or to yourself. Yes, speaking negatively to or about yourself counts.

Criticism coming from your mouth about you still hurts. It's you feeling disappointed by you. It's you degrading and demeaning you.

Have you thought about why?

What is it that makes you feel the need to degrade yourself?

Do you even know?

Was this a learned behavior?

Did someone close to you teach you how to belittle yourself?

The way that you talk of yourself when no one else is around is the greatest indicator of just how you feel about yourself. The things that you think and then allow yourself to bring to life in this realm is key to the value that you have placed on yourself.

It is this value that you have determined that you are worth that can lead you down a pathway of destruction very early on in your life.

The feeling of unworthiness has caused many to fall prey to self-destructive behaviors that has caused irreversible damage to your core.

You have allowed yourself to be tricked into thinking that these destructive things that you are doing is fun. You know getting high is fun, wrong. Getting high in no way makes you feel better in the long run because the impulsive attitude you have developed towards the negative and condescending words that you have allowed to penetrate the core of you have left a void so deep that you think this is the only way to fill it. So, you surround yourself with people who feel and do the same. You do not want to be corrected nor do you at this moment want to be helped. You have even fooled yourself by rationalizing why you deem this negative behavior good for you.

You lie repeatedly to yourself in a last-ditch effort in response to the criticism that you face daily. Every time you look in the mirror at yourself, you are reminded of what you have failed at, refusing to see what you have succeeded at.

The negativity has mounted in your life in a way that has you afraid to seek anything positive because you feel unworthy.

It is the repetitive nature that you have developed towards the negative that has you craving it, so much so that whenever someone gets close enough to you to start trying to deliver the positive you immediately reject it.

The mind is an amazing creation and unfortunately when it is corrupted with the negativities that happen in this world it is very difficult to get it out. Now the heart on the other hand is a reservoir of holiness when you are operating in the will of the Most High. Your heart is programed differently than the mind. They are at some points in time operating independent of one another. This is why you must be very careful about who and what you allow in both because the corruption of the mind is negative but the corruption of the heart is catastrophically sadistic. The heart is the core of a hue-man being and also of a spirit being dwelling within a hue-man beings body.

The heart is a magnificent creation and mighty in its own right because it can still live when the brain dies. That's why the heart is protected more than the head is in the physical. See, as long as the heart is beating the other organs in your body can still function. If the heart goes so does every other organ. A bullet proof vest was created to protect your heart from harm in the event of a gunshot. The bullet proof vest is used in essence to stop the heart from being penetrated by a bullet or another sharp object directed at the chest region. The heart is amazing to say the least. It is even able to survive outside the hue-man body long enough to be transported and surgically placed in another hue-man being's body.

The brain however isn't set up that way. Up to this date there hasn't been a successful brain transplant and if the heart stops working so does the brain, although this is not the case with the heart because it can live even when the brain is dead.

The brain is not the focal point when total corruption is being spoken of from a spiritual standpoint. The brain however is at the forefront when speaking of the first steps in the corruption process.

It is at this stage that you are being told negative things that go against the positive blueprint already embedded within your brain. The loving, caring, happy moments that make you smile. You know the things that made you feel warm and carefree until tragedy and trauma struck.

It is usually the first experience with trauma that scars you the most. This is the first layer of destruction, the first layer of self-criticism, the first layer of doubt. It takes only that one time to permanently scar you for life.

These initial scars can cause you to abandon everything that you were taught to be right/positive and take up the wrong/negative things to do. The way you handle and view the first trauma is paramount to the success or failure in holding onto the promise because it is difficult to see the promise when everything you were taught before the trauma now looks like a lie. You were taught that good things happen to good people. So why did the bad happen to you? If you are good. You weren't taught about the beasts that live in this world with the good people. You weren't taught that the beasts even look similar to you and even if you were taught, that's why it is hard to know just by looking.

There are certain things that your parents neglected to tell you because of fear and there are other things they didn't because they didn't know.

Depending on when you were born there just are certain things your parents weren't allowed to talk about because it was considered taboo and they learned this from their parents who taught them that all things will just work themselves out which clearly is not true.

All things in life requires you to do something in order to get something in return, nothing and I mean absolutely nothing just happens or just works by itself. This sort of thinking alone causes trauma. Yes, you just sitting around waiting on something to materialize out of thin air, keep waiting and let's see how that turns out.

It's like wishing for a baby but you don't want to have sex and you don't have the funds for the sperm bank nor invitro. So, what do you do? Oh, I see the baby will just be left on your door step one day. Now that is a possibility but highly unlikely. The point that am making is you must do what is required to get what you want. Sitting around waiting only gets you loss of time and further away from your desires. The promise is yours to fulfill and the journey is not without pain and agony, disappointment and heartache.

As long as you are living in this world you will have to endure some unspeakable things for the sake of progress to purpose because you are not here on this planet alone. There are other's and they have their own agendas as well. Keep that in mind as you navigate through this terrain called life on this planet.

Not everyone is against you but not everyone is for you either. You must learn to be dependent on you and raise your expectations for yourself and lower them for others because they don't have the capacity to reach the bar that you set for them. They aren't you and your capacity for evolution is more advanced than theirs. Keep this in mind as you allow people into your zone. Also know that not everyone will accept your rise well. There are those that secretly want you to fail and they aren't strangers, they are the ones that you call family, friends, and loved ones.

These are the people who smile in your face and frown behind your back. The ones who throw shade on every bright event that happens in your life. You know the ones that say, "are you sure you can do that?" When they know that you can, they just don't want you too because it, whatever it is, doesn't coincide with their plans of you. Beware of people who claim to love you but are always throwing the cloak of doubt on everything you do because that surely is not love.

Be mindful of the company you keep because everyone in your presence is not there for your betterment. Some are there for your demise.

« CHAPTER 16 PUNCTURE »

A puncture is a seemingly small wound caused by a sharp pointed object. These types of wounds can easily mask something far more serious than the natural eyes can see. Some of these wounds are also necessary for the purpose of healing, which is why there comes a time in your life when you must deflate. Yes, I mean literally put a hole in it, to let the air out of negative situations, so that all of the crap that you have been unnecessarily going through can stop. You must stop all of those people and their problems from adding to your wound.

Ask yourself why do you refuse to puncture that infected wound?

Is it because you want to keep the toxic relationship?

And if so why do you want to keep something that clearly isn't good for you?

You keep expecting the rising to go down on its own instead it keeps getting bigger. Unbeknownst to you all you have to do is puncture it so that everything inside that doesn't belong can come out. The situation that caused the rising in the first place was an unattended problem that needed your attention that you failed to pay attention too. Now you're in a state of panic because what use to be normal is now abnormal and you are afraid to do anything to fix it.

Outsiders have told you that ***"it's nothing major just leave it alone and it will get better on its own"*** but your body keeps telling you different.

You have chosen to listen to the advice of the outsiders instead of your spiritual insider. This action alone has caused you to swell with infection in every area of your life. Your refusal to puncture those infected areas in your life has you filled with pain.

The pain is an indicator that something deeper is going on. It is the bodies response to something that is wrong.

Are you listening?

I mean are you really listening to what your body is saying to you?

There is always a cause to everything. Nothing happens without a reason. Thus, the cause-and-effect.

Cause and effect are relatives to events and things where one is caused by the other. For every action, there is a reaction. This is balance. Everything that you do has a consequence, it will either yield you positive or negative. It is up to you.

When you make the choice to carry other people's burdens without regard for yourself, knowing that you have your own burdens to carry, what do you expect to happen?

You know that you are already overwhelmed by the things that you are going through that you haven't effectively dealt with yet, yet you purposefully have decided that you will add to the already heavy burden by bearing someone else's crap.

Now don't get me wrong, it is good to help other's when you are in a better position to do so. Unfortunately, at this current moment you are not in the position to do so.

Your number one priority at this moment is for you to help you. Your quest is to get you to a healthier place where you can better serve yourself. It is this service of self that will guide you to your happy place and in this happy place you are going to see the true you. The you that no one else has ever seen because she has been hidden under all the layers of scars that she bears.

You have an obligation to yourself to do whatever is required to get you to a better state of being you. No one else can do it except you.

There are layers on top of layers that you must go through to get to that happy place. It is imperative that you discover the hidden you. The you that you are afraid of. The you that wants what's best for you right now.

You're filled with so much pain from your punctures that you think that it's normal when in fact it is not. The hidden you tries constantly to reveal that to the unhidden you but you refuse to adhere.

In those moments when you are alone and you laugh out loud from a place of happiness, soon after you feel a sense of guilt.

Why?

Do you even know?

You are so full of the pain from all of this negative mess that when those small glimpses of the hidden you appear you quickly push her away because you feel unworthy of her and all that she brings. Your pain has become your comfort and you want to hold onto your comfort even though you know that it is not positive nor good for you.

The pressure is mounting and this is causing an already hostile environment to become even more hostile.

What is it that you truly want?

What will it take to get it?

Do you even know?

Stop and examine the current state that you're in and ask yourself those questions because they are important to your healing process.

You must learn to gain a better prospective on all things you and with greater clarity.

It is the clear and concise analysis of yourself and the situations around you that are going to lead you to the answers that you seek. These answers are relative to the point of action that's required to gain the prospective that's needed to propel you into your destiny.

Your destiny is being held up by your refusal to do what is required. The initial pain that you will suffer from the first puncture is nothing compared to the lifetime of suffering that you have already endured. This self-inflicted wound is mandatory for the healing of the root of you because it is going to relieve the pressure from that lifetime of buildup.

Yes, it is scary. Yes, it will hurt. Yes, you will see things that you don't like. Yes, it will be unpleasant. Yes, you will live through it.

You have already gone through your worse, so don't keep sweating over the small stuff and allowing it to manifest into something that will negatively impact you for the remainder of your life.

Deal with the little things immediately as they come. This will allow you the freedom to navigate your terrain without the boulders because you have already taken care of the pebbles.

Dealing with the mole hills before they become mountains is the key to a smoother journey.

Trust in your abilities to be the greatness that you seek and once this greatness is achieved know that it doesn't have to be achieved again.

Make sure that the heights that you plan to go to are not unnecessarily repeated because it is this that causes you to second guess yourself.

Remember that greatness once achieved leads to greatness once deceived. It is this achievement that pushes you to a greater sense of deception by fooling you to keep pushing for what you already have obtained.

Once you have obtained certain heights stop and take a closer look at them so that you don't repeat them. This is a waste of time.

You are the greatness that you're trying so desperately to achieve.

« CHAPTER 17 QUESTIONS »

It is an absolute shame that we live in a world where being a black woman is not acceptable for black women. However, it is acceptable for any other woman to pretend to be a black woman and it is even a deeper shame that it is even more acceptable for a black man to exhibit hate towards that very black woman who gave birth to him then turn around and pretend to be her! The her that I speak of is the BLACK WOMAN. We meaning black women are the only and I mean the only women on this planet that are told on a continuous basis that it is not okay for us to be us. From the suppressing of our hair to the degrading of our bodies to the humiliation of our features, until they are worn on someone else's face that is.

We black women have been hated for being the supreme being since time came into existence. Man made sure that they flipped the script and created the dogma that woman came from man. They fabricated the story and made it seem as if woman came from within man when the truth is that man came from within woman. There is no woman on this planet that was born of a man, however every man on this planet was born of a woman.

So, in essence when you hate the very woman that gave birth to you then you hate yourself and your very existence. That's why you try so hard to erase the black female so that you can feel a sense of entitlement when in all actuality you should feel shame. Shame to the point of repentance because you would not exist if it weren't for that BLACK WOMAN.

You even try to argue the facts and twist things to fit your own selfish needs. For instance. The word SHE even tells you that you came from within **SHE**. Remove the S- then you are left with **HE**. See He came from within SHE and in order to get SHE from HE you must add S, however with SHE and the removal of He is a taking away from that which is already in existence. The same goes for WOMAN, WOMEN, and FEMALE. Even with conception and birth, man is placed within the WOMAN and birthed from within the WOMAN. Woman is the incubator for man and woman, not the reverse. So, in man's pettiness to become superior they tried to twist the truth to fit their own desires.

Not even realizing that in their quest for Divine power they have created a ripple effect that will cost them dearly. It is no secret that we all have our own parts to play on this planet and when you try to take on the role of someone else you create chaos and this chaos has caused the very favor that is to be obtain from God through the black woman to be held up. This is the reason for the destruction of the black man and until the black man learns to stay in his place and accept the truth he will forever be on the most endangered species list. This chaotic state has also caused the black woman to bear the burden of playing both roles in the household and creating in her the disappointment of having the carry the continuous weight of the fallen black man. This disappointment is often mistaken for bitterness.

The black woman has high expectations for the black man because God has high expectations for her. She is the link between God and man. She is the portal by which every man on this planet has made his entry point. She is the housing for all life forces. She opens her gateway for man to release and if his seed is approved she allows it to navigate through her galaxy with the hopes that the supreme being will reach the planet and plant his seed for nourishment and growth in her fertile environment. She then cultivates, nurtures, and carries it to term. She is the link between life and death. It is she who decides to do or don't. She who carries, delivers, feeds, and cares for that which she has been allowed by God to be the creator of.

It is the worldwide crisis of the extermination of the black man that has them blinded by the lies of who they are and why this is so. It is not knowing that has both the black woman and the black man in bondage right now. It is through the retraining of the mind and the doing what is required that truly changes things.

The value of the black man has fallen to the value lower than that of a dog, no pun intended. It is a proven fact that you will get away with killing a black man quicker than you would killing a dog. It is the lack of unity and self-knowledge that hinders the black man from excelling and those who do achieve do so with a warped sense of self, dictated to him by those with hidden agendas. He walks around with a false since of self with a white woman on his arm shouting black power and I am King. When the truth of the matter is, he is a pawn, a peasant, and a phony.

It is the whitewashing of the black woman and the black man that has bridged a gap so wide that only Divine intervention is needed to fill it. During this whitewashing, the black woman and black man have been brained washed into thinking that they are this new creature called mixed. When in all actuality they are simply a lighter version of black. Listen, BLACK is DOMINATE and everything else is recessive therefore you can never erase black, you can only dilute it.

Black people are the true HUES. The true rainbow of color ranging from the very dark black to the very light beige. All colors come from us. So, there is no way possible for us to be the inferior beings.

The sad reality is that the black woman can't heal the black man until the black man stops wounding the black woman.

God made the black woman to be the filter for the black man and in her lack of knowing she is unaware of her role in the black man's life. She doesn't know that the comfort and healing of the black man rests in the lap of the black woman and when the two finally do join physically neither is fully aware of the roles that each one must play so the purpose of the two joining can't be fully met. The black woman hasn't been taught the proper way to be spirit led and neither has the black man.

They are unaware as to why they behave the way they do because they haven't taken the time to get to know self. They are so caught up in being physical that they aren't in touch with being spiritual. They see everything as one dimensional. They only operate in this realm and are totally oblivious to the other's. So, the lack of knowing gets passed down from one generation to the next.

Black women are loud because for generations they haven't been heard. She yells out of frustration trying to get you to listen to the fact that there is a problem that she needs your assistance to solve. Yelling for her has become her last resort because nothing else she has done has gotten your attention. You have not listened to the settle cues that she has given you that indicate something is wrong. She yells because her expectations of you have not been met. She yells because she is disappointed. She yells because she hasn't been allowed to do what she was created to do and that's to filter you. She yells because nobody wants her to be her, not even you.

The black woman is frustrated while melanated. Labeled as an angry black woman when she has every right to be when everyone has benefited from her being the black woman except for her. She has been forced to lay with someone else's husband in the presence of her own husband because the owner of the husband refused him that night and she has bore babies of this rapist against her will and has been forced to feed someone else's seed from her breast before she could even feed her own bastard seed. Then to make matters worse she had to cook, clean, bathe, and be humiliated by the very woman who forced her to do so and the black man who promised to protect her and the white man who raped and impregnated her. The white woman has been constantly uplifted while the black woman has been bearing the weight of everyone else's crap on her shoulders. The black woman has been carrying the black man, the white man, and the white woman for generations just to be called a lazy bitch and a hoe.

It is the constant humiliation of the black woman that has led to her aggressive behavior that of which has become a stronghold passed down from one generation to the next. The black woman has no place on this planet where she can go for comfort not even in the arms of the black man. So, she yells out of frustration because it has now become her battle cry. Her yells are mistaken for anger when it is in fact a cry for help, a cry for relief, and even a cry for redemption. The black woman even in 2017 is still the most disrespected woman on this planet. She is the only woman taught from an early age that she doesn't need a man and that she is independent, thus in it all alone.

The black woman has cried out of pain to be heard and yet it has all been in vain. She has developed a condition called hatred. She hates herself because everyone around her has told her that she is not worthy of any better treatment. She is mocked by society and must constantly fight for the right to be her. She is fighting to wear her hair the way it grows, her nose the way it shows, her lips full, shiny and thick, her voluptuous backside the way it rises and the wideness of her hips.

It is a shame that the only way for the black woman to be glorified is if she is a he, wearing a dress. It is more acceptable for a black man to dress up and pretend to be a black woman than for the black woman dressing up to be herself. The black man is even respected and praised for pretending to be the black woman while the black woman is disrespected for being a black woman. Where is the logic in that? This is absolute madness. Insanity even. The black woman is then forced to pretend as if she is someone else to feel worthy. It is a problem that continues to grow because of the lack of knowledge and unity amongst black women.

Even the discrimination amongst black women has created a whirlwind effect that keeps us further divided by skin color. Where the dark skinned black woman has a problem with the lighter skinned black woman because they feel as if the lighter skinned black woman has been treated better and has had more opportunities for advancement because they have a lighter complexion. Then you have the lighter skinned black woman who has a problem with the darker skinned black woman for believing that she has it better.

It is all because we, meaning the black woman, hasn't come into the complete knowing of who she really is. It is all shades of black that make us who we are and it is the coming together of all shades of black that will deliver us from where we are. We must first, one by one gain an over-standing and a knowing of self through study and self-examination.

Who are you?

What are you?

What makes you think the way that you think?

What makes you do what you do?

What makes you feel what you feel?

What makes you like what you like?

What makes you dislike what you dislike?

Do you have the answers to any of those questions?

If not, why?

It is senseless to boast of knowing another being and not knowing yourself.

Do you even know why you keep attracting the same type of spirit?

Do you know why you haven't received what you have been praying for?

Do you even know why you keep giving to people who don't give you anything back in return?

Do you know why you keep falling into the "it is more blessed to give than it is to receive" syndrome?

Do you even know why you are more comfortable giving to other's than you are giving to yourself?

Do you know why you feel guilty when you laugh out loud when you are by yourself?

There is plenty of studying to do on yourself and it must start now because before you can move forward you must truly know thy self. Knowing these simple things frees you to start knowing the rest of you. You can't keep making excuses as to why you don't know the answers to the questions about yourself.

Look you go to school and work hard to learn all the lies that they teach you but you won't even put in a tenth of that time to learn anything about yourself. Those schools that you attended didn't teach you anything about yourself as an individual nor as a group. You were only force fed their lies and handed a cookie and some milk during lunch time. You didn't learn anything about your spirit being nor the adequate things about your physical being.

However, they did embed in you a desire to be someone else because everything you learned was about someone else. You were taught that someone else was better than you. You were taught that you should follow their rules, so that you can go to their schools, so that you can get their degrees, so that you can get work in their companies, so that you can live in their houses. You were taught how to be the modern-day slave. You were taught how to be ***CONTROLLED***!

The sad reality is that you are even comfortable with the way things are until a black man is shot but even then, you are afraid to do what is required to bring about adequate change. Yeah, I know you march and yell for a few minutes then you go right back to your master's rules. The change that is required must happen before a black man is shot.

Doing what is required has nothing to do with you doing your best because your best is not needed in this equation. You must learn to allow your spirit to guide you to making the necessary steps to lasting change. This process will not be comfortable and it will not be easy. It will require you to retrain your mind and body. It will require you to do what is ***REQUIRED***!

You are required to know what your place really is and to stay in it no matter what. You can't get what you can't give. You want change, then change. You want to be treated better, then treat yourself better first. Everything starts with YOU!

You must come to a point in your life where you are able to do what is required of you to develop into the purposeful you. The you that doesn't try to force people to stay in your life, the you that is truly comfortable with the necessary changes that must be made to complete the task at hand.

No one is responsible for the choices that you make except for you. The woman that you must be must come from within you. She is not outside of you and you pretending to be someone else will not help you on your quest to be you. Emulating and copying someone else is not being true to you. You were created to be different, unique, and set apart. So, why do you keep trying to be like someone else? It is a great disservice to you and everyone else around you. No one will be true to you until you start being true to yourself.

There must come a point in time where you must come one on one with the spirit that dwells within you and when that time comes you must comply. That body is just housing for the spirit in order for the spirit to function in this realm. The spirit needs to be seen, heard, and felt and being within you allows the spirit to do so within this realm. However, when the flesh does not comply with the spirit trouble is soon to follow. By trouble, I mean the negative aspects of life.

The black woman must learn to be holy while on this planet and she does that by allowing her spirit to navigate through this terrain called earth. To guide her to that point and time where she will receive the other part of herself. That point and time where she will become fused. It is the process of fusing that will allow her to see her entire being from beginning to end. She will then know why she had to go through the things that she had to go through. It was all for the greater good which is love. There is no greater love than that of self and when I say self I am speaking of all facets of you. The other parts of you that make you total.

Stop focusing on what the next black woman is doing and start focusing on what you need to be doing for self. It is the studying of self that is going to get you to that space in time where the fusion will take place and every time you stop doing what is required for self, you delay getting to the fusion process.

Everything in this realm is about timing. That's why time is our greatest resource and once it is gone you can't get it back. There is plenty to do before the fusion process begins. You keep praying for change when you are not ready for the change that you seek. You have not even begun the necessary work on self. Those questions that I asked earlier in this chapter you still don't have the answers too, do you?

« CHAPTER 18 REMNANT »

What is it that you have left after the trauma? "Pieces of you, you say." Not knowing that the pieces no matter how small are still significant enough to be put back together again.

You in your pain have decided to discard the remnants because you think that they have no value.

Every piece of you is vital to your survival in this realm. Even if is it as small as a grain of sand, it is of importance because it is all of those remnants that make up the totality of who you are.

Yes, things have happened to you that caused you to tear into tiny pieces but if you would allow yourself the necessary time to gather all of those pieces and put them back together again you will see that the brokenness didn't take away your value.

Nothing that you have gone through or has happened to you can change the fabric that you are cut from. You will always be a God directly linked to the God. Your heritage is directly related to The Most High God and no one can take that away from you.

Your self-worth and value aren't determined by the things that have happened to you nor is your chosen path. You must keep this at the forefront of your mind no matter what is happening around you.

You being a factor from the God's has you at an advantage without you even knowing it.

This advantage as fortunate as it is also has you at a disadvantage when it comes to demonic/negative attack. There are forces that know your worth even when you don't and they prey upon it. You not knowing you puts you at a greater disadvantage when it comes to being traumatized.

You are in a constant state of chaos when you don't know who and whose you are. This lack of knowing leaves you at risk for even more trauma. The pain will keep coming as long as you keep allowing the disconnect between the natural you and the spiritual you.

Your focal point has to be you at all times because when it's not, you keep allowing the remnants to slip by you.

When you keep missing these key pieces you will eventually suffer a loss that you can't regain thus having to unnecessarily repeat the process.

This missing of pieces and lack to regain them is what causes you to miss the mark when it comes to your destiny.

Everything and I mean everything is about timing and when you aren't gathering what is required to complete the task this is a sure way to miss those golden opportunities when they arise. By missing those you also miss timing. See, the timing that is required to be at the right place and the right time is dependent on several factors but all of those facts depend on you.

You are the key component in everything that surrounds you and knowing this fact is also important because there will come a time where you will need everything you to pull yourself back together when the pieces are torn away.

In this society, most are taught that their value is brought about from their service of other's and this is not the truth because your value has absolutely nothing to do with the next being.

Your value was set long before you entered into this realm. Your value is far greater than anything in this realm and any other because my dear you are PRICELESS. No one can change that and just because someone calls you a worthless piece of crap doesn't mean that you are and news flash even crap has a value, it is not worthless.

Don't crap for weeks and let's see how much it's going to cost you. Better yet ask the people who use crap as fertilizer for your food how much it costs them.

The point that I'm making is that everything no matter how insignificant it may seem has a value to it and it doesn't change just because you aren't aware of it.

Everyone and everything has its part to play on this planet be it positive or negative or the role of both. The dual role is often played by all of us at some point or another in our lives it's just that most won't admit it.

The doubt that you bring into your equation is brought about due to your inability to trust your core self, the spirit that inhabits you. This action is a negative one. This alone causes traumatic events to unfold in your life because you have now become a magnet for others to come along and do you the same way that you do yourself.

Yes, you! You created this behavior by mistreating yourself and not trusting the God within you. You fell into the trap of only trusting in what you can see and that in itself is a façade because there is no way hue-manly possible for you to trust someone else when you clearly don't trust yourself. Love is the same way. You cannot and I repeat cannot love anyone if you don't love yourself and if you don't love yourself how can you expect anyone else to love you? I'm just saying, how?

I have talked extensively about you setting the tone for the way other's treat you and I will keep saying it because it is a fact. The people in your life learn how to treat you based on how you treat yourself be it conscious or unconscious, you are the teacher.

This is why self-examination is important because it shows you why certain things are the way that they are, why they happened, and how to fix them if need be.

Your duty to yourself is to awaken from the physical, psychological, and spiritual slumber that you're in. You need to be at all times from henceforth conscious because a conscious black woman is so powerful that when she enters an environment she takes over it. Everyone and everything in it must comply. She is the embodiment of strength and Godliness and there is none like her. She is regal and knows it and she is not afraid to show it.

A conscious black woman is feared and with great reason because she is the root to the black man. She is the only one that can awaken him from his slumber and subconsciously he knows this. For a black man that's not ready even sees the very help meet created for him as a threat and will try to rip at her core. Yes, the unawakened black man will try to tear at the fabric of the awakened black woman.

It is fortunate for her that she has been trained for this during her awakening process. The black man will not succeed in his sleeping state to destroy the black woman because she has been equipped to stop him.

In all of his ripping and tearing at her, she has refused to let up and back down from her quest to bring her man out of bondage. She knows emphatically that if he is not awakened soon everything that was promised to them will go unfulfilled. The quest of the black woman and the black man rest on the shoulders of the black woman. The black woman on her quest to assist the black man in his awakening process has left her with deep scars. Scars that the typical sleeping black man can't see. It is only when the black man awakens that he is even able to see the scars that she has had to bare because of him.

The world has painted this picture of the black woman being this weak lazy timid worthless individual who just so happens to be last on the totem pole, according to them.

It is this misconception that has caused the black woman to doubt her purpose for being before she awakens. Fortunately, with all that has happened the black woman even asleep still senses that something isn't right. She knows that the behavior that she exhibits is contrary to what she feels within.

She has even in her slumber picked up on settled cues from her spirit but has dismissed them as mere figments of her imagination.

The black woman contrary to what the others teach about her is a very loyal being and loyal to a fault even. It takes a lot for the black woman to give up on the black man because she knows that he in all of his strength and glory still is not the strongest of the two. He may want society to think that but it is not the truth from a physical, psychological, nor spiritual stand point. The things that the black woman has had to endure just during child birth alone is a clear indicator of that.

No matter how the black man pumps his fist in the air or flexes his pectoral muscles, he is still not the strongest vessel overall. The black woman for the sake of the black man has had to hide her strengths from him so that he wouldn't feel inferior. She pretends that she can't do certain things so that he will feel needed. She takes the blow of the spiritual licks just so he won't feel certain pain. She protects him in ways that he can't even fathom, even if he knew.

The black woman standing with her shredded remnants wondering what happen to the unity that was promised to her. Wondering what happen to the spirit man that she bore. The black woman with all of her battle scars cries out for more. More love than lies, more harmony than hate, more relative than refusal, more worthiness than worry, more happy beginnings than unhappy endings.

The black man yearning in all of his might wanting the black woman to awaken him from his lack of foresight.

The black man sub-consciously wanting to be held down by love but afraid of showing his vulnerability to the very black woman that he needs. The black man out of fear runs from the very black woman that he knows is the key to his awakening. He knows that she is his third eye opener. He knows that she is his builder. He knows that without her he is destined to stay asleep. He knows.

He also knows that her remnants as small as they are holds the answers to both of their predicaments. He knows. He knows that if he doesn't get his crap together and soon that they both will have to come back here to this planet and do it all over again. He knows. He knows that it is because of his inability to comply and unwillingness to do that has them of both in turmoil. He knows.

The black man has even taken pieces of the black woman's torn pieces and used them for his own benefit to hold her hostage and delay her from being able to fully assist him. He knows.

The black man has made excuse after excuse as to why he has belittled and demeaned the black woman that holds his blueprint within the confines of her fabric. He knows.

This very black man has left his conscious black woman to dwell within the caves of the snow hoes, pretending to be conscious while using the term black power as if it were the keys to unlock the doors of the caves that have him in bondage and even caged.

The mental bondage that the black man has undergone has not just affected him but the black woman and the black children. In his absence, they have suffered tremendously in silence wondering when will it all end and when will the black man take his rightful place beside the black woman.

It is not the black woman's place to stand behind the black man. Her place is beside him and his place is beside her. Not back to back but side by side. There is unity in the showing of both of their faces at the same time. It is this simultaneous act that leaves the other's in fear because this action of oneness solidifies both the black woman and the black man as a unit. This magnifying effect creates a ripple in the fabric causing whatever that's negatively sitting there to be removed. The ripple and waving is actually cleansing. The cleansing of what's no longer needed and the opening up room for what is.

Some of your remnants can be better used elsewhere and that's okay too because it is up to you to decide what to keep for your mending process and what not. Just be careful not to get rid of something that's imperative to your healing process.

There are certain things that you negatively create by being naïve.

« CHAPTER 19 SCRATCH »

This is to the black woman in all her glory I say to you scratch. Scratch that itch that's been bothering you for years. You know you want to.

It's been a long time coming where you were able to get to that spot, you know that spot that you use to try to get someone else to scratch for you and they never could get the scratch part right and that frustrated you to no end.

Well I tell you now that I know your secret, yes, you. The secret that you have been afraid to utter to another hue-man being. I know that you long to be with someone else. I know that you married the wrong man. I know that you didn't stick to God's plan.

I know that you hate certain parts of your life. I know that you even dread being his wife. I know. Now take a deep cleansing breath and scratch that itch. Make sure you do it gently.

Today I honor the being that you are by telling you that it's okay to feel whatever it is that you are feeling because it is necessary.

It is necessary for the betterment of you that you take this moment and acknowledge that you messed up more than once and you regret it and if you had it all to do over again you wouldn't. It's okay. I know.

I know that it hurts you every time you think about the wasted moments of your life that you can't get back. I know that when you look around and see what should be yours, it hurts. I know that every time your skin grows over your scratch you scratch it again and it hurts.

I even know that with all of the money that you have you are still that scared little black girl crying out for attention and still don't get it and it hurts.

I know that with the beautiful face and the thin waist you still don't like yourself. I know that at night you muffle your cries so that no one else can hear. I know every time that man that you vowed to love, honor, and cherish is close by you can't stand his presence.

I know, I know, I know.

It is an unfortunate thing to be so angry with yourself that you literarily scratch layers of skin off your body and even dig holes in yourself.

The disappointment that you feel has you at an all-time low and now you're wondering how are you going to come out of this.

The bad choices you made for what you thought were good reasons now have you stuck in situations with no seemingly good way to come out. Fortunately for you there is a way out and your negative choices can have a positive output as soon as you learn from them.

It is the lessons learned that have the greatest impact on the quest to the true you. Learning is a part of the process and these lessons no matter how painful still bring about a greater sense of self.

When you keep striving for your dreams, you know the ones that keep coming into your conscious and subconscious, there is an unquenchable desire that will not go away until all of your dreams have been fulfilled.

Those restless nights and that feeling in the pit of your stomach that won't go away are all part of the process to fulfillment. It is your inner being pushing you to do what is required so that you can move to the next level.

There is so much to be done and little time to do it in. You have no time to waste, every moment must count for the positive. There are so many things that you have yet to scratch off your to do list and in doing so those things that are slowly being removed are for your betterment. Although some of them don't feel like it because of your desire for them but trust that in the long run you will see the benefit.

Often when you are going through any type of removal in the beginning it seems like a loss because of the missed placed value you put on it. You have from an early age saw value in people and things that no one else did because of the God in you. Unfortunately, this has caused you to trust in people and things that weren't supposed to be trusted. You always saw only the good aspects so much so that when the bad aspects started to show you refused to see it. You kept saying that it was just your imagination yet again, when in fact it was not.

The high expectations you have for others has them at a disadvantage because they aren't capable of achieving it even if they did try. Just because you see the good in an individual doesn't mean that they do and just because you have placed a higher value on them doesn't necessarily mean that it is what they are worth. You yourself have often been in stores where you have seen overpriced items that weren't worth the price tag placed on them.

Did you make notice of it?

Did you contemplate buying it?

Did you buy it?

Did you make mention of it to someone?

Did you ask them to buy it?

Well that's the same way it is when you over price someone or something in your life.

Is it really that valuable to you?

If yes, why?

With all that you have invested, are you even getting a return on your investment or are you taking a loss?

These things should always be considered because it is your life and everyone and everything should have a value placed on it but in doing so make sure that the value is just and fair.

Now ask yourself, is it placed at the fair market price?

Or have you inflated the price to make other's think that it is more valuable than it's worth?

Yes, there are some that would say that no hue-man being has a price because we are all priceless. In a way, this is true. However, there is a value placed on the placement that people and things have in your life. No one in your life should be held at a placement higher than yourself.

Knowing your worth and setting boundaries is essential to the betterment of you. This allows for healthier relationships within and outside of you. There will always be things that will come along and have you questioning what you know is right. During those time's you must stick to what you know to be the right thing for you. Don't fall into the trap of thinking and feeling something just because someone else does. Think for yourself and research what you aren't sure of.

For example, most black women are taught that all black men cheat which is not true. Although a large percentage do and most of them do it not even aware as to why?

The average man doesn't know why he cheats, he only knows that he does and that society has embedded in him that lie that it's in his nature to cheat. However, it is not in his nature. A man cheats because he is searching for the other part of himself. He sub-consciously doesn't know it. There is this spiritual magnet that drives a man to search for the being that is the other side of him and there is nothing that you or anyone else can do about it. He will keep searching until he finds her. His quest is not meant to directly affect you nor to cause you harm although it does when you allow yourself to become romantically involved with him.

The black man on his journey to his true black woman will along the way stop for a treat and unfortunately that treat is any woman that will allow him to relieve his pressure.

He callously goes about dumping his seed in his temporary treat thinking that it's harmless and then he moves on. This is his way of detaching himself from the event and shielding himself from any feelings that he may have, be it negative or positive.

The black man driven by his heart's desire may make many mistakes on his quest to find his one true love. Sometimes he isn't aware that he is causing you pain. He just wants to be comforted until he finds her. Even when the black man is aware of his maltreatment of you he sometimes still doesn't know how to articulate what he is feeling. He doesn't know how to say, "I am lonely and afraid that I won't find her and can I play with you until I do." Yes, be it harsh or not it is his truth.

The black man in his unawaken state will not be truthful to you or himself for that matter and even the awaken man will still be afraid to tell you the truth for fear of judgment and rejection. He still needs someone to allow him to make pitstops along the way without attachment.

I am in no way condoning the black man's behavior. I am actually trying to get you to a place of overstanding why certain things keep happening to you. The black woman has become a magnet to certain types of people and behaviors because of her past. It is these things that has her pinned to a certain board for all to see. Those attracted to her who are like this comes from a deeply rooted place within her that's been tainted by the past events that have happened to her.

The black woman and the black man have scratched themselves until they have broken several layers of skin trying to ease the itch that ails them. These scratches unfortunately aren't just physical in nature they have surpassed that and embedded themselves into the spiritual core of them.

The scratching has now become a catalyst to a bigger problem. It is now being used as a purposeful way to cause pain. You now scratch not to alleviate the itch, you now do it to cause the pain on top of the itching.

You in your unwillingness to again listen has caused an even wider gap in the pathway to your purpose. The black woman and the black man are both at fault for their own part in this mess.

Trying to minimize the magnitude of this issue has created another issue. Can't you see it? Every single one of you have a role to play and every single one of you know that whether you admit it or not. Some just don't want to do their part but they will take the credit once the task is completed by someone else.

Cheating is not the biggest part of the problem. It's the endangering of the cheated on one's life. Now that's really a problem. On the black man's quest to find the black woman that's cut from the same cloth as him, he inadvertently and carelessly does things that puts the temporary woman at risk for dis-ease and trauma and the future permanent black woman.

In the black man's quest, he must keep in mind that his journey albeit his is not just about him. Yes, I stated that you must put yourself first but in doing so do not endanger someone else's life. If your need to scratch has caused you to make reckless choices and you become infected it is your duty to let the person that you decide to make a pit stop with know that you are infected. There is no non-disclosure when it comes to protecting one's life.

In lieu of all that I have said, you have a moral obligation and in some places a legal obligation to tell a person you plan on having sex with, whether protected or unprotected, your health status. You are living in a time where having sex with someone is about your life and your death, literally.

Your quest, no matter how difficult it is, does not give you the right to hurt, harm, and endanger someone just because you are hurting. Yes, you are to put yourself first in all aspects of your life however, "remember no harm, no foul."

When you come into the realization of who you are there are certain things that you just won't do anymore. Like have sex with someone you know you aren't on the same vibrational levels with.

Don't let the urge to scratch knock you off course. I know that you are lonely. I know that you have needs. I know that you think no one over-stands. I know that time is running out. I know that you are tired. I know that you feel like giving up.

I know that this is the time that you must be extremely careful because having sex in the state that you're in could possibly be more deadly than any disease that you may get or give. It may just cost you your spirit because when you are having sexual intercourse with someone you are actually also embarking on a spiritual exchange with that being.

Sex has very strong spiritual implications and when you have sex with someone it bonds you to them physically, psychologically, and spiritually. This sexual act of spiritual exchange can have a very negative impact on you and your future Divine partner. This is one of the main reasons why sex with anyone other than your Divine partner is not advisable.

Most people when thinking of sex only think of the aspects of two bodies interacting and one penetrates the other but what they don't look at is the fact that more is happening during this seemingly simple act of intercourse. These two hue-man beings are engaging in a sexual act with spiritual implications. So, if you are God's positive energy and decide to have sex with satan's negative energy, what do you think is going to happen? Although the two of you may look to be similar beings doesn't mean that you are.

There are times when you unknowingly engage in acts with those that are not your kind and when you are made aware of it you get mad. You know deep within you when something is not right yet you keep going after it anyway. That itch wants to be scratched and there are moments when you don't care how it gets scratched as long as it does.

Desperation has caught us all slipping at one time or another and for those of you who have never been caught by desperation, "I say, keep living."

The need to scratch at times does become so intense so much so that it requires assistance. Yes, it does.

You know you have had someone else scratch for you plenty of times. The physical scratching was the easiest, right. But did it make you feel better? Oh, only for the moment, right.

The things that a hue-man being will do to get temporary satisfaction without regard to the long-term effects are surely at an all-time high. Some would call it selfishness but it isn't, it's lawlessness. They have no regard for the law and I am speaking of the spiritual laws.

These spiritual laws are set to keep you from physical, psychological, and spiritual harm. The sad reality is that most people aren't even aware of the spiritual laws that affect them every moment of every day. Spiritual laws are nothing like the physical laws that govern the lands that you live in. They are far more simplistic than those in the natural yet hue-man beings in their ignorance, when awakened still refuse to follow.

The spiritual laws are simple, love. Love is the law of the God's. There is none greater than the infinite power of love. The laws to love yourself comes first in this realm because when you truly love you there are certain things you will not do again.

Self-love is the greatest honor and praise that you can give to God because when you are operating in love for yourself there is a certain way that you will behave towards yourself and towards other's.

This also carries over to that desire to scratch. When you scratch with the intent to love you do so lovingly.

It is not rough, brisk, nor rash. It is gentle, kind, and meek.

The handling of yourself and other's changes to that of positivity without the need for negativity and it shows.

You will shine in a way that other's will see the glow of God on you and want to partake in it. Just be careful not to share to the point of depletion and always share in a way that leaves you revived and rejuvenated.

That need to scratch may always be there but the urgency may differ. In all things you do, whether a black female or a black male, do it with the mindset that it must be for the greater good in a positive way, no matter what.

Know that there is going to always be positive and negative aspects to every part of the life that you live but it's your choice which side you want to dwell on.

Certain things will come up but it's how you handle them that will cause a negative or a positive reaction from you. Things do come and catch you off guard and in those moments remaining calm is the last thing on your mind but you must do so. Remaining calm in a chaotic situation can help you make better choices and save you from further trauma.

Staying focused when that intense urge to scratch comes is very difficult when those around you keep pressuring you to do the wrong things. I've said it before and I will keep saying it.

You are anointed and favored and set apart therefore you mustn't fall into the trap of doing what other's do. Your mindset is to be different from those around you. You were created that way for a reason. You are a God created to lead and the sooner you realize that the better things will be for you. Stop trying to conform to the will of other's and do what is required of you.

Your main focus while on this planet should be on building a more effective relationship with your spirit.

« CHAPTER 20 TATTOO »

Did you know that a tattoo is just a pretty scar when healed properly? There is an estimate of more than 3 billion people worldwide who have tattoos and as pretty as some of them can be, they can also be ugly and dangerous.

There are various reasons why a person may decide to get a tattoo and very few know the roots cause of this choice. Most think it's because of the beauty of it and some as a statement of something symbolic to them. Whatever their conscious reason is, it is far removed from the subconscious reasoning.

Everyone who has a tattoo has experienced a great amount of pain receiving it and no matter how many times you are stuck with that tattoo needle in most cases, it is just as painful as the first stick.

A great number of people while undergoing the tattooing process are under the influence of something to help alleviate the pain, be it alcohol, illicit drugs, prescription medicine, etc. Then there are those who want to feel the pain of the tattooing process so that they can mask another type of pain that they are already going through. As strange as that sounds it is the truth for some people. There are some who actually welcome the pain and in their pain, it is a release of sorts for them.

In some places around this world it is a taboo to have a tattoo, so those that do live in those regions of the world hide them so they don't have to deal with the stigma attached to it.

It is also known that tattooing has the ability to become addicting but is it really?

Or is it the pain associated with the tattooing process that's really addicting?

There are some people who have been preconditioned to have addictive behavior and when they undergo the tattooing process this triggers those pain sensors that have been damaged because of previous trauma and sets in motion the pleasure sensors as well.

It is because of the past trauma that they now associate pain with pleasure but is it really?

Or is it creating a greater pain to cope with a lesser pain?

There are those among us who in their conscious mind have tricked themselves into thinking that if they could just cause more pain to themselves then they can somehow feel better about the first traumatic event.

Most on the surface can't articulate how they're feeling to anyone else so they find alternative methods to cope with the pain from the traumatic event.

When looking at a person that has their body almost completely covered in tattoos I often wonder what happen that caused them to be in so much pain.

Everyone handles their pain differently and rightfully so. Tattooing is for some an acceptable way of coping be it conscious or subconscious.

As with all things that appear to be good there is always a down side. There are many people who die from infected tattoos but it is not televised because the ratio of deaths is minimal compared to the ratio of those who lived through theirs. The risks that are taken do not outweigh the benefits for those who want the tattoos and most don't even take into consideration the risks at all.

The society that we live in casually looks at themselves as risk takers without considering the actual consequence of the risk itself.

Some of the people who have tattoos would vehemently deny they have ever been traumatized and rightfully so because it takes a different kind of person to publicly admit to having undergone such horrors in their life, especially at a young age. The truth of the matter is everyone at some point or another have been traumatized by something. Some people just mask it better than other's.

The fact of the matter is, whether the trauma is known by other's or not, it doesn't take away from the fact that it happened. Even if the person it happened to has the ability to block out the memories from the conscious, the subconscious still knows.

The skin is one of the largest organs that we as hueman beings have yet the average person doesn't know it and because of this lack of knowledge doesn't treat the skin as an organ. Most just say it's skin but it is far more than just skin because of the abilities that it has.

The skin that you have has three layers.

1. The epidermis is the outermost layer of skin and provides a waterproof barrier and skin color.

2. The dermis is beneath the epidermis and contains strong connective tissue, hair follicles, and sweat glands.

3. The hypodermis is composed of fat and connective tissue.

Each layer of your skin has a function and each function is of equal importance. When you tattoo your skin, you are altering the first and second layer of your skin, this is why the ink stays and also the reason for the tremendous about of pain.

It's amazing what the hue-man body can do for you without you even realizing it. Did you know that your immune cells immediately go to work on your behalf to fight the foreign substance you call ink that you put into your body while getting the tattoo and that for the rest of your life your immune system will keep fighting for you and protect you from the ink that it sees as a threat and a danger to you and every time you get another tattoo your body has to work even harder to keep you from harm because of the ink?

No one I know has ever explained that nor do they know it to even explain. You do things and don't know the ramifications of the action that you have committed.

All you know is that it's pretty and you like it but you have no clue as to the damage that you have caused because of it. We all have this lack of knowledge in many areas of our lives that leave us damaged without knowing until something else comes along and forces us to learn.

Every time that needle penetrates your skin it causes a wound. Now think about how many times you had to be stuck to complete the tattoo and now imagine your body being covered with them and the fight that your immune system has to constantly do to keep you healed. Now look at that from a psychological standpoint. Now look at it from a spiritual one.

Every time you go through a traumatic event in your life your body signals for help and the immune system goes to war on your behalf and you aren't even aware of it. It doesn't matter which area it's in.

Everything always no matter what it is goes back to spiritual warfare. There is always a battle going on and there is no such thing as normal and as long as you try to fit into a category that doesn't exist you will keep failing. We are all unique beings created to be DIFFERENT! So, stop trying to be something that you're not and embrace your differences because they are what make you, you.

It is you that has made things harder for you than they have to be, by not allowing what you know to be right to reign. Yes, again, here I go, your spirit. The biggest battle is being fought for you by your spirit so stop making it more difficult by not adhering.

« CHAPTER 21 UNDERLYING »

Has it been recently brought to your attention that you are the underlying cause of all of your issues?

You have been given the opportunity every day that God allows you to open your eyes to evolve. In every given moment, you always have two options, to step forward into the positivity of growth or to stay still in the negative delusion of safety. You think that just because you stay the same that that is somehow better than changing.

You have been doing a great disservice to yourself by pretending to be the same person you were ten years ago. You have changed but the change hasn't been one of betterment. The change isn't positive nor is it productive. Everything you have been doing has been counterproductive to your Divine purpose. You have been going against your chosen path because of your unwillingness to accept the reality of your spirituality.

You are fighting against forces stronger than the physical you and you know that this battle is a spiritual one yet you keep using physical things to fight with and have the audacity to think that you can win with them. It's like taking a gun and shooting at a spirit.

There is always something bigger behind the issues that you are dealing with and the healing that needs to take place is within the changes that you need to make.

Taking the first steps to change for the positive will initially hurt you very deeply because it is uncovering the issues beneath the surface. There is always a reason even when the reason is not apparently known. This is why studying yourself and the events that led to the initial trauma are important. The findings will lead you to key pieces to your puzzle that's needed to see your journey from a greater prospective.

The scars left behind from the trauma are not just on the surface but when you see them your only focus is what you can see. The average hue-man being looks at things from a one-dimensional view and are not taught to go beyond that.

Your happiness on this planet is not contingent on you pleasing others but rather on you pleasing yourself in a way that is befitting to the God within you. Honoring that holy part of yourself will teach you to honor that hue-man part of yourself and vice-versa. You keep saying that you are the daughter of a king but never speak into being the daughter of a God. The true and living God for that matter. You never walk and live as God's daughter. You never see yourself as God's daughter. You never behave as God's daughter but contrary to all of that, you are God's daughter. You are the daughter of The Most High God. Now live with that. Walk in that. See in that. Be in that.

I on this day honor you and every day after this, I honor you and I pray that you on this day learn to honor yourself.

No issue, no matter the size, can change who you are on the inside. The fabric of you is intact and you must learn to see that.

Have you ever heard the phrase, "if it was meant to be then it would be?"

Well let me enlighten you on a few things about that. First of all, there were a lot of things that were meant to happen in your life but because you made the choice to do something different or go left instead of right you missed the opportunity to receive.

You and your underlying issues have stopped you on more than one occasion from receiving your blessings. You have even forfeited some of them. You have inadvertently made a lot of people happy by turning over to them what was rightfully yours because you refused to listen to your spirit. It was meant for you! All of it! But you wouldn't do what was required because you didn't feel like it. You missed the mark because you weren't at the required place.

Sometimes it is your underlying issues that increases the fear that drives you to second guess doing what is required.

As you navigate your way through this earthly terrain keep in mind that other people can and will suffer because of your negative choices. What you do does have an impact on other people and the sad reality is, it is those you know and those that you don't. Complete strangers can suffer due to your negative choices.

The impact that your underlying issues have on you and those that you come in contact with can have deadly consequences. Those choices that you make due to the underlying issues are done because of the disruption in your ability to think and function clearly. The pain and agony at this point has caused you to inadvertently look for others to inflict pain upon. The sad reality is that hurt people cause the most pain to others. **"Hurt people, hurt people."**

Those that are caught in your chaotic mess aren't initially aware that you are this damaged because on the surface you appear to be intact and what they deem to be normal, which we all know that there is no such thing as normal but let's just use the word as an example of the labels that people place on one another. It is this name placement that has so many people chasing after things and people that aren't right for them. These titles have encouraged people to lie, cheat, steal, and even kill in the name of titles.

It is often looked at as the be all to end all when you have that title by your name. It is looked at as honorable and even prestigious in this realm however your titles and prestige have nothing to do with your spiritual responsibilities.

The work that you are required to do in this realm needs to be done with you being in a state of true awakening. The awakening process requires you to deal with the underlying issues that you have been hiding for so long. Just because you refuse to deal with them doesn't mean that they will magically go away. You must at some point confront the things that haunt you and the only way to do that is to take the first step and stop running. You have been running for so long that you actually think that you aren't actually running.

You have conformed to the ideologies of society and deem everything that they say and do to be correct. You don't check for yourself. You have allowed them to tell you that you have no issues and therefore there is nothing that you have to repair about yourself because you are in their category of normal.

All people at some point or another develop some issues in their lives and some make the choice to deal with their issues immediately and there are others who refuse to admit that they have any issues at all.

It is apparent that as long as you are in denial about the source of your issues you will forever be struggling with your healing. Everything is up to you because you are the only one that can fix what is broken within you, so stop waiting on someone else to come along and fix it for you.

Learn to release what has you unnecessarily captive to negativity. You are the source of everything that's required to guide and lead you on this journey. Trusting in your abilities to do what is required must become your anthem as you forge ahead on your quest to be the you that you need to be.

You have the power to speak life into any underlying issues in your life and you have always had the power to do so, you just didn't consciously know it.

The change that you seek and even sometimes crave is already within you, you just need to learn the necessary steps required to bring it out.

« CHAPTER 22 VITIATE »

Vitiate means to make faulty or defective, to impair or to make ineffective, to debase in moral or aesthetic status.

Even in your broken places there is still value to you. The things that you have gone through didn't render you valueless nor incompetent, so stop confusing worthless with worthy and vice-versa because you are worthy and not worthless. Just because your circumstances may seem bleak doesn't mean that you don't have the power to correct them.

Negativity is just displaced energy. You are energy and a magnet to whatever you are feeling so be careful what you disperse into your atmosphere.

Your personal environment must at all times be filled with positivity because it is this positive energy that's going to be the safe haven for you when you come home from a long day of dealing with the negativity that bombards you when you are out around others.

Your circumstances already have you at an all-time low and the disadvantages that come along with that can quickly become disastrous.

You're caught in a whirl wind of indecisiveness trying to figure out how to correct the wrongs and move forward. In all of your efforts to correct and move forward you have attracted the very brokenness in others that you are trying to avoid within yourself.

The mirror of life is reflecting back to you what you are in your state of brokenness and because of your pain you can't see it. It has even rendered you ineffective in many areas of your life. Now you are walking around existing instead of living the life that you were meant to. In your ineffective state, you have become the walking dead. Everything about you speaks death although you appear to be alive. You walk, talk, and breathe but there is no sign of life. The truly Divine living that you were meant to live when you entered into this realm is not apparent. You get up every day pretending that all is well when you know that it isn't.

Just because something isn't readily made available to you in your discovery process doesn't mean that you should give up on what you know is a part of your destiny. Sometimes things aren't available at that time because you aren't ready to receive it. When you are given access to things or people when you aren't ready, you don't value it nor them the way that you should. Some experiences you go through actually prepare you for what you've asked and prayed for, so that when you do receive it you will appreciate it. For example, it's like thirst and hunger, you don't know thirst and hunger until you've been thirsty and hungry. Some things you must experience for yourself because sometimes experience is the best teacher, especially for the ones who refuse to listen.

Some people will see another person go through trauma and laugh, then turn right around instead of learning from what the other person went through then find themselves in a similar situation due to the fact that the warning signs were over looked because they thought it couldn't happen to them.

Most who are in the beginning stages of any type of trauma are in a state of disbelief and rightfully so. Even the highly intelligent find themselves at some point in their lives victims of circumstance. The circumstances that surround most traumatic events are brought about because of the refusal to govern your thoughts. It is the negative mindset that sets you up for negative situations. Remember you are what you think if you think it long enough. That works for the negative and the positive.

A positive mindset can change your circumstances also. You want to be a winner then you must think winner. Yes, it's just that simple. Hue-man beings tend to complicate every aspect of their lives by wanting others to do what they should be doing for themselves. Even when it comes to prayer. They will ask for prayer and not even pray for themselves and when they do pray they think that it is something magical that will fix everything instantaneously, without them having to do anything for themselves. So, they sit around and wait and wait and wait for their prayers to be answered when they have the ability themselves to make some of the things happen by getting off of their butts and doing what is required. Other than prayer, what are you doing to fix your own situations?

You ask God for things that you have the ability to get for yourself but you don't want to do what is required to get them. You just want something to fall out of the sky and that's not how it works.

Your prayers are ineffective because you are praying for what you have the ability to get for yourself and God knows that. Everything requires that you do something even if someone says they have something for you and it's free. Free really isn't free when you have to use your car, gas, and time to go and get it. See, you still payed a price although it wasn't for the item itself, you did however pay to get to the item. I will even break it down a little simpler for you. Anything that you use your time for is being paid for, so in essence nothing is free because your time has a value attached to it.

Despite the things that have happened to you your ineffectiveness is actually an illusion because nothing can stop you from doing what you need to do because of who you are. Stop falling into that trap of impaired faultiness. Nothing and no one has the ability to stop you from doing anything that you want to do.

Yes, there are wounds and scars from the battle but there is hope and the ability to conquer everything negative.

You are far stronger than you think and you must learn to stop focusing on the negative aspects of your life and do something about it. You have the power to turn any ineffective situation to an effective situation.

You have the power to take anything that seems bleak and turn it around to complete. Over and over again you must keep reminding yourself of the necessary steps that you must take to get to where you need to be.

Also keep in mind as you make progress in your journey know that some of the people that are with you now will not continue with you. So, when the universe rids certain people from your life it's a blessing and although it may hurt, you can't lose anything nor anyone that means you good.

It is apparent that you must set boundaries for everyone in your life including yourself so you don't fall into the trap of ineffectiveness again. Don't keep allowing other's to negatively influence your behavior towards yourself. You must allow yourself ample time to grow into your state of positive effectiveness. This requires you to change certain things and people in your life. You can't keep negative people around and expect to remain positive.

Negativity is like a virus and it grows. If you have to keep telling a person that's directly involved in your life to stop bringing negativity to you, then this is a person who doesn't respect the fact that you have placed boundaries on your relationship with them and they should be removed from your life.

Stop giving access of your life to people who don't respect you and stop making excuses for the way you handle them. You have set the tone for their behavior because you do it to yourself. You say right in front of them that you are going to stop the negative behavior and before the day is up you are in their face saying, "let's do it." It doesn't matter what the it is because if it is negatively affecting your life it needs to go.

You are only as effective as you want to be and that goes the same for being ineffective.

Everything and everyone surrounding you needs to be strategically placed so that you know who and what to remove when the time comes because the time will surely come. As you grow out of the negative behavior you will attract more positive people to replace those that you had to discard because of negativity. ***Remember everything is about cause and effect.***

« CHAPTER 23 WOUNDED »

They say that imitation is the greatest form of flattery, but is it really? People say things without any regard as to why they say them. We live in a world where the average person wants to be anyone other than themselves. Their main focus is how to copy, immolate, imitate, and pretend to me someone else. They find it easier to pretend than to be authentic.

They even choose people who they turn into an idol and start to worship them not knowing that they have made that person their God. The sad reality is they aren't even aware of the God in them. They want so badly to be a part of someone else's fantasy instead of properly functioning in their own reality. Not seeing that these people that they idolize aren't exempt from wounds nor scars. We all have them. No matter the financial bracket or the popularity status.

Be careful who you make the choice to idolize because the role model you have decided to pattern yourself after may be worse off than you. What's shown on the outside is different than what's behind closed doors. Make sure you dig beneath the surface before you mimic someone else's lifestyle.

When you make the choice to deny who you are and try to take on the personality and image of another hue-man being you have no idea what dangers you are placing yourself in.

Everyone has their own battles to fight and with fights come enemies. When you want so badly to be a part of someone's life because you think that their life is so much better than yours, I say beware. You just may be opening yourself up to a legion of demons. Their negative energy and aura may be too much for you to bear.

With new levels come new devils and everyone has an agenda.

You must always take into careful consideration that just because a person has more than you materially/financially do not mean they have peace of mind nor happiness.

The wounds that they bear may not be apparent at first glance because some wounds are embedded so deep within that it takes time to get to see them.

Some people are very clever and good at hiding the wounds that they bear so it may take a lifetime of being with them before you will even see them. The scars left behind from the trauma that they experienced may have even caused them to split into multiple personalities. I am not talking about where when you are home you are one-way verses being out in public. I am talking about a clear and concise psychological disorder.

In all of us there is the need to be more guarded when out in public than in the privacy of our own homes. So, when you see a public figure or celebrity for that brief moment and time in public you only get to see a very small fragment of who they want you to see. Anyone can pretend for a few moments. It is the moments spent alone indoors with a person that you began to see small fragments of who they really are.

The trauma that you have experienced at some point in your life is what shapes and molds you as to how you present yourself to other's in this world and it's also the trauma that attracts certain people to you as well. You inadvertently give off a certain energy when certain things have happened to you that's left you scarred.

Every hue-man being comes to this realm with their own energy and aura and the things that traumatizes them has the ability to change the energy and aura that they came to this planet with. The way a person handles the traumatic event is paramount in the healing process. Some traumatic events depending on the person can render you totally useless to yourself.

Wounds no matter the kind nor depth is something that must be treated immediately to ensure that a life is not wasted trying to self-medicate so that you don't feel anything, especially the pain.

As spirits having a hue-man experience there are things that can't be avoided and can't be explained. Some things just are.

There is this unfortunate lineage that you have when you enter this realm and that has nothing to do with you per say but everything to do with the people that you chose to be your parents.

You came to this planet already damaged because of the two people who procreated together. You were conceived in misunderstanding, strife, lies, greed, and deception. You inherited the strongholds of those that came before you and you wonder why you can't get certain things to go right.

You have been plagued by certain dis-eases and ailments to no fault of your own. You have also been plagued by the negative attributes of both parents. These negative things have left you at a starting disadvantage.

Some conceptions aren't created out of love and happiness nor peace and harmony. Some conceptions are created out of violence, hate, rage, and malice. These negative things are passed on to the child along with of course the positive things from the parents no matter how small.

This is why it is important when given the choice, to carefully research the person that you plan to procreate with. You will not find out everything but try to find out as much as possible about him and his family because they are the ones that are going to be passing down both positive and negative properties to your children.

The black man is responsible for passing down certain negative aspects to their children and then refusing to take responsibility for it.

Be mindful of the black man who smokes the blunt and drinks his henny before bed. The marijuana and alcohol remains in his system for an extended period of time and become a part of him, this is then released into your system within his sperm cells. You may not have ever taken a drink of alcohol nor a drag of marijuana in your life but your child created with this man has now inherited addiction because that's what it is. Oh, you thought it was so cute that he could blow a ring of smoke with his blunt and down a whole bottle of henny in 30 minutes tops, until your child grew up and started doing the same thing. Not to mention the violence and abuse and the lack of responsibility. Yes, they can be passed on to your offspring.

Some of the wounds take a life time of constant care to ensure that it doesn't infect the entire body because sometimes there is no healing, only dealing with and maintaining are the only coping mechanisms.

Then there are those times when you are the source of your wounds because you won't let your spirit do what is required and therefore your spirit will make your body sick to get your attention.

Your spirit depending on the depth of the reasoning behind the mission at hand will shut you completely down in the form of certain dis-eases and illnesses so that you will have the time to reflect and hear what is being transmitted to you from within.

For every trauma and life altering event you were warned. Yes, it was that deep feeling you got in your stomach, that nagging feeling that just wouldn't go away, the dreams that kept coming. You felt it before it manifested in this realm but you casually dismissed it.

Your spirit did what was required but you failed to do your part and now you are wounded and mad. You are now filled with hatred and that hatred is misplaced and directed at the wrong people. Deep down inside you know that you are the blame, you are at fault, you just didn't listen.

The lessons received from not adhering is just as painful as the scars left behind. You have now changed forever and trying to navigate your way through the bumps and bruises isn't as easy as you were told it would be. Now your quest includes learning how to live with the new wounds and merging them with the old wounds, as you get back on course from the detours that you have taken. Nothing can totally prepare you for what is to come and unfortunately there is nothing you can do to change what has already happened, but I implore to you keep trying no matter how difficult the road ahead may seem. There is always a chance to do what is required while you are still alive. Use this day to prepare for what you have asked God for and smile because the hardest part of your journey is already over.

All set backs are a set up for a great come back.

« CHAPTER 24 X MARKS THE SPOT »

The vagina is a portal (lock/door/gateway) and the penis is a vessel (key/stick/wand).

The vagina is an electrical outlet.

The penis is an electrical cord/plug.

The one and only true and living God is the energy source/power supply.

Man needs to insert his plug into the woman's outlet in order for him to feel the full current/power of God and thus become totally useful in his purpose.

When a man is linked with the right woman (the woman that God created for him) his time in the portal/outlet becomes one of charge, regeneration, peace, comfort, healing, and most importantly love.

The black woman is a filter for the black man. She is the only one that can filter and soothe him from the outside in. She has been created by God to use her portal to rejuvenate her man.

She accepts the task by pulling/milking all the negativity from him that he encountered during his hectic day when they join as one. It is the merging not just of two bodies but also of their spirits.

When she allows her man to enter her sacred space he is to be at rest/peace. This is the rest in peace that is often confused with death, it is really the resting of peace in life/love. She is to drain/draw from him in order that he may be freed from the burdens that he has carried.

She is then to release those burdens to the Source/God and the Source/God then takes those burdens and recycles them and then gives the new Spirit filled charge back to her for her to give to her man.

Oh, wait there's a catch. This can only be done with the right person and when you take your time and allow yourselves to be totally taken in by what you are feeling and doing at the same time.

With each stroke, it must be deliberate. The thought of the stroke must be made before the stroke. You two must be so in tuned with one another that you are thinking of the same thing at the same time.

Eyes open, lights on, look into the eyes of the one you love as you slowly stroke and then gently and slowly stroke and then gently and slowly stick your tongue into each other's mouth. Do not break the connection because it is needed for the total refueling of the Spirit and body.

Kissing is very important to the refueling process because it is the completeness of the circle. The fusing of the two from portal to portal and the only point that the woman can enter the man.

The point where there is no separateness. Where the spirit can totally take over and fuse both bodies into one.

As this is happening be sure to slow down your breathing along with your thrust/stroke and remember to think about every stroke before you make it. The slow and more deliberate the thought and stroke the more intense and stronger the climax/orgasm.

Woman as the man is thrusting/stroking make sure you use your vaginal muscles to pull him towards/in you as you both are stroking in unison. Also, as he pulls his thrust back gently push along with him by releasing the vaginal muscles. The vaginal muscles and thrusts must be on the same vibrational rhythm as his in order for this to work.

When you both start to reach your orgasmic peak slow your breathing down more to a deep in deep out along with each thrust. Inhale and exhale, slowly thrust, whine/stroke, kiss, and grab one another buttocks gently.

Now man slowly release, woman hold yours. I know it's right there, don't worry you'll get yours as soon as he finishes releasing. This is vital to his healing now as soon as he finishes you milk him by slowly clamping down with your vaginal muscles then slowly release and let the orgasm go. That's it now climax. Keep whining slowly as you continue to kiss one another. Make sure not to break the bond right away. Allow your Divine partner to stay within your portal until your breathing is back to normal.

When the woman is being sexed properly she is revitalized and it is nourishment for her body and her spirit.

That oneness brings about healing. It is an elixir/medicine for her. Research even shows that the more a woman has sex and is ejaculated inside of the happier and more at peace she becomes and is better equipped to continuously filter her black man. The sperm itself medicates her by producing a calming effect.

The flip side of that is once sex is withdrawn or denied the black woman goes through withdrawal and depression because she is not able to do what is required of her spirit and that's to filter her black man. The other part of herself.

The black woman and the black man have the ability to heal one another when they are on one accord. The black woman and the black man were created to complement one another physically, psychologically, and spiritually.

The spiritual exchange is one of holiness and power and when done the way that it is intended it is a glorious event and one that the God's honor. Sex is first spiritual and then natural. Sex and its power of holiness is even wanted by demon's and this is the reason for the sexual violence and perversions that run rampant in this world.

The vagina in its awesomeness is a portal to the world beyond. The vagina is a place of holiness and demons even know it. That's why so many young children are raped and their innocence taken away. It is far deeper than the anger of a rapist, it is the cutting off of the holy vessel needed to filtered the chosen ones, the black man. See, the black woman can't filter the black man when she isn't aware of her powers or who she is and demons know that. So, when a young black girl is raped and grows into adulthood she is incapable of using her portal for the holiness that it was intended for until she recovers from the initial trauma of the first rape.

The journey to all power rests in the fact that you must learn all there is to know about who you are and your purpose for being.

You are the essence of greatness even in your broken state. You must learn to heal yourself so that you can do what is required of you to bring the black man to his complete state of awakening so that he can be what God intended for him to be. He can't reach his full potential without you and the reason he wants sex all the time is because it is how he rejuvenates himself. He isn't even aware of the reasons because he thinks it's about getting some but it's far deeper than that. It's all about the release and the refill. The releasing of the negative energies/toxins and the refilling of the positive energies/auras of Godliness.

Sex in its state of naturalness is only one dimensional but the Spiritual Exchange is multi-dimensional and heals all that ails you.

So, when women say that all he wants is sex you are right and wrong. Yes, he wants sex but in the form of the Spiritual Exchange that's needed for him to complete his assignment on this planet. He needs to enter you as often as possible so that he can be refueled to handle the negative/demonic forces that burdens him on a daily basis. So, when he is going without sex or having it with the wrong person or people he is damaging his God factor and slipping further into the hue-man factor. Constantly losing touch with the spiritual side of himself and forgetting that he is a spirit of holiness having a hue-man experience in this realm.

The black man doesn't know how to articulate the words required to explain to you what he needs from any perspective in his sleeping state. It is only when he begins to awaken that he starts to listen to the instructions of his spirit and even then, it is difficult for him to tell you for fear of rejection. He may even be fearful that you will think he is crazy just as he thought you were when you tried to awaken him when he wasn't ready.

The subconscious of the black man knows the spiritual reasons why he needs to have sex often, it's just that the conscious doesn't.

The black man needs to enter the black woman's portal as often as necessary so that he can stay focused and spiritually tuned.

The black man cheats and hunts for sex because of this reason. He is on a quest to find the right portal and he will stick and move as many times as he has to too find her. The sleeping black man only knows she's not the one when he enters her and the awaken black man knows once he sees her.

Sex for both the black woman and the black man is far deeper than the conquest or the notch in their belts when they're awakened. It is about the healing of the bodies for the merging of the spirits. The spirit needs the joining so that both pieces to the puzzle can reunite and do what's required to leave their mark on this planet and return to the state of limitlessness, where time doesn't exist and everything is in harmony with complete oneness.

The spiritual exchange is a very powerful tool used in conjunction with the spiritual elements that merge all the realms together. It is like nothing of this world when done in concordance with holiness.

Ladies don't get too excited about knowing this because there's a downside. The black man in his hue-man-ness will run from you when he initially realizes that you are the one because he is afraid. You are the only one on this planet that can shut him down literally and figuratively and he knows it. You are his weakness and the black man in his hue-man-ness doesn't want anyone to know that he has a weakness, not even you. So, he will run and go find someone that he can pretend to be strong and invincible with. Someone who appears to worship him without him being accountable to her. Someone who makes him feel like a King instead of the God that he truly is and it's okay for him because he doesn't know that he's a God yet anyway.

The black woman in her awaken state unknowingly makes the black man feel like crap because she knows that he truly is a God, despite his behavior when he doesn't. The black man even in the sleeping state knows that he is not worthy of the black woman in her awaken state. Although he tries to make her feel like it's something wrong with her being awakened.

When it comes to your touch he can only take it for so long because the longer he receives it the less control he has and this is a clear no, no for him.

The black man is taught from an early age that he is the man and thus must always be in control of everything and everyone around him, especially his black woman.

He is reared to be hard and emotionless. **"Told not to cry and when he's hurt to suck it up because**

you're a boy and boys don't cry." This statement alone damaged his core and he tries his best to live up to those false expectations of him for fear of being labeled as weak.

The black woman in all of her essence tries to cope and is often misunderstood to the point of giving up especially when it comes to being spiritually sexual. She oftentimes has to hide who she is so that the black man can feel a sense of comfort when he is intimate with her. She is left feeling empty and void when she should be overjoyed and elated that she was somehow able to filter her man but it never happened because her man is still that wounded little boy who was told not to cry. The same little boy who lives in a grown man's body and enters her with force and thinks that beating the vagina up is a term of endearment when it really is degrading and disrespectful. The unawakened black woman lets him because she thinks that is the way it's supposed to be so that he can be happy.

There is no happiness in letting anyone pound your body like it has no value. The Spiritual Exchange is about gentleness and the merging of the spirits and that can never be done in the mist of brutality. Most black men don't even realize that only a black woman who is in her sleep state of not knowing will let you do her that way and that this sleep state is prolonged because of childhood sexual trauma. She in her pain will allow you to inflict further pain hoping that it will take away that pain from her first traumatic sexual experience. Oftentimes she is pretending to like the brutality of your thrusts just to get it over with. Most black women who have been sexually abused as a child have a difficult time having an orgasm, if ever.

Sex for some is a turn off and for others they become involved in deviant sexual acts like the ones that were performed on them as children or they go into the dominatrix acts of sex because it is deemed as powerful, it's their way of taking back their stolen control over their body by controlling someone else's. Sadomasochistic sexual relationships are dangerous physically, psychologically, and spiritually. This type of sexual relationship is about demeaning and belittling the man that hurt her and it doesn't matter that you weren't the one who did it because in her mind all men are that way. When she is allowed to treat him this way it gives her an illusion of power over her abuser and the scariest part is the man who is willingly involved in this type of sexual relationship was also abused as a child and more than likely by a woman. This is why he seeks women who will gladly oblige him. It's a dangerous game to play with neither party coming out a winner.

This is some of the reasons why it is best to research your partner. Find out as much as you can about their sexual history especially regarding abuse because trauma of this magnitude can cause problems in your relationship if not dealt with immediately.

« CHAPTER 25 YOU »

There are some that would like to debate about who they are while on this planet and never think to study who they were before their entrance into this realm. Everything in this realm can be traced back to who you were before this time came to be.

You are and have always been in existence even before time came to be. You are infinite! Your spirit that is. Your spirit has been with God since the beginning of the beginning. ***You my love are a God!*** You are created in the image of your creator. Which makes you a creator.

You are the essence of individual unique perfection. There is none greater than you.

There must come a time when you see yourself as you are. You are a God first and everything else second. Stop allowing society to dictate how you see yourself and who you are. You must get to a point where you know without a shadow of a doubt who you are, whose you are, and why you are here.

Your outer appearance is only who you are in this realm. It is your spiritual energy that your focus should be on.

Society teaches you that outer beauty is paramount when it is in fact the opposite.

We have been disillusioned by societies idea of beauty and what's important. Society would have you think that there is no such thing as spiritual beautification. Spiritual beautification has nothing to do with the outer beauty because your spirit is energy. Spiritual beautification is about love and the more you truly love the more beautiful your spirit becomes. Your spiritual power increases and your sense of self heightens.

When you learn more about your spirit being you become more in tune with the natural part of self. It is this harmony that is essential to the development of complete unity of spirit and body.

It is the need for the body to control that hinders the spiritual process. When compliance is done in a timely manner the spirit can share the power with

the body in a way that leaves the body spiritually awaken.
You begin to adhere to the heightened sense of spiritual awareness and focus more on the spiritual aspects of this life rather than the natural.

Your knowing of spirit first becomes the foundation of all things you.

You start to search for the real meaning behind and in front of everything by analyzing self and all things you.

Your focus shifts to solitude and isolation during this time of self-discovery because you are now aware that distractions are disastrous delays.

These distractions are negative energies sent to throw you off course. That's why the process of elimination is a must. You must learn that eliminating people and things from your life during this time is paramount to the success of your mission. Self-discovery can be a more painful process when you have people and things in your life that devalue the work that you must do on self. You must stay focused on the task at hand.

This journey of self-discovery is not just for you. It is for those who have been assigned to you. You must learn so that you can teach those that have been assigned to you.

It is the lack of knowledge that has you hindered and it is the knowing that will free you.

That body that you have is hindered and limited in a way that the spirit is not. Therefore, the spirit can navigate the body in a way that the body can't navigate itself.

When total alignment comes the spirit and the body are better able to navigate in this realm and do what is required to fulfill the mission at hand.

You are a key element in this vortex and it is essential that you realize that.

You must realize that your return to this realm was a mandatory one. It was a must that you be here in this space and time. Since time began you became a time traveler. Moving from timeless to time trying to connect with the other part of your spiritual self.

There is another hue-man being that houses the other part of your spirit. The flip side to your coin. The ying to your yang.

It is the driving force of love that has you continuously returning to this realm. ***The love of self.*** See, although a part of your spiritual self is being housed by another physical being it is still you. The spiritual you that is.

God, the ultimate creator created every being in pairs. You are not and never have been alone. You are a part of great Godliness. You are a key piece to the Alpha and the Omega and the time has come for you to walk in that knowing.

Stop allowing the deflated mindset of society to brainwash you into continuously thinking that you are less than when you are far more than they will ever be.

You are a quintessential part of the Divine's plan for restoration and healing of the chosen ones. That's why you go through so much negativity, hardship, and heartache. These are things to keep you distracted from knowing who you truly are.

The weight of all the negativity has you rethinking what has already been shown to you in the spirit. You doubt yourself and your purpose based on the negativity that society has burden you with.

You feel alone and left out because the weight of the burden is difficult to bear. The other part of you appears to be hidden so you settle for a temporary replacement to help you bear the burden only to end up with a heavier load to carry.

The impatience causes you to make choices that you know are not right for you thus causing you more pain and anguish.

You refuse to do the work required to become the change that you seek and blame others because of the choices that you've made.

You have even overlooked the settle cues that your spirit has shown you in an effort to save you from yourself.

You keep dismissing what you know to be right and settle for what you know to be wrong for you. Punishing yourself for wanting better, for wanting all of you. The you that your spirit keeps showing you.

It is not an accident nor a coincidence that you are feeling the way that you are feeling, experiencing the things that you are experiencing, and dreading what you are dreading. You do not need to go outside of yourself for the answers to your questions because they are already within you and once you start accepting who you are and what your purpose is then things will become more apparent to you.

When you keep denying the totality of self the uneasiness will continue and the dissatisfaction will remain an active part of your life while on this planet.

Your quest to connect to the other part of you is actually easier than you think.

It is your denial of self that has you disconnected from doing what is required to bring about self-totality.

Every time you deny who you are by not adhering to your spirit you push yourself further away from complete oneness.

All you have to do is listen and do what is required. By listening to your spirit, you are one step closer to achieving what you deemed to be impossible.

Once you start truly listening to your spirit and start doing what you were guided to do then you will start seeing the results manifest.

Also keep in mind that the results that you will start seeing are the results that the spirit wants and the results that the flesh needs. So, don't get discouraged when what you see doesn't look like what you expected. Remember, this is about the internal first and the external second. Spirit then natural.

Will the results be instantaneous, maybe, maybe not? That is up to you. You decide how fast or how slow your results will be and that is determined by when you do what is required.

No one else holds the keys to your destiny except you.

Yes, there are others who will play certain roles in your development but you are the key player.

The other part of you is also required to do what you are doing. You are being guided to one another by forces far greater than you know and it is up to you how fast or how slow the process will be based on your choices.

The choices that you make are affecting both parts of you and it doesn't matter that you are not physically together yet. That's why you are feeling what you are feeling.

That's why you have all of these manmade achievements and no true happiness. You have equated a mass accumulation of things with happiness. When in all actuality it is the oneness that you seek, even if you don't know it.
The emptiness and loneliness will still persist while you are in a room full of people pretending that all is well when you are dying inside because there is this sense of incompleteness hovering over you.

You have everything materially but lack true oneness with self. So, you keep using your money to comfort you and that's always short lived because as soon as you purchase the item you feel empty all over again.

Now you have started to misuse people to fill your void and that's not working out either because as soon as you are done the emptiness is back. Oh, wait my bad it never left because while you are with the person you are wishing, hoping, and dreaming of being with the other part of you. You just needed a quick fix to tide you over just in case tomorrow isn't the day that complete oneness will come.

It's a shame that your act to fill your void has delayed complete oneness from coming. See, every time the need to fill the void becomes overwhelming that's when you are close to achieving complete oneness of self.

If you would just endure that moment victory is sure to follow because complete oneness is about timing. Yes, you being in the right place at the right time is paramount and you can't be there if you are distracted by something and or someone else.

Allowing the flesh to lead will cause you to fall prey to destiny killers. Those that have set out to stop you from achieving complete oneness and they are very much aware of your gift and mission on this planet, even when you aren't aware.

They sometimes come clothed and dressed in the finest. Seemingly to be the desires of your heart. However, this is furthest from the truth.

There are always negative forces at work just as there are positive forces and you must be aware of both because the two work simultaneously in your life.

You do have the power to choose which one will reign in your life by allowing your spirit to reign supreme.

A negative mindset will never give you a positive lifestyle because you become what you think.

« CHAPTER 26 ZERO IN ON TARGET »

The black woman is an open target of mismanagement and maltreatment throughout this world and yet one of the most emulated women on this planet. She is secretly envied and valued above all other women in this world. Yet publicly told that she doesn't matter and have no worth. This is all part of the illusion of the others to make the unawakened black woman feel inferior.

In the United States of America, they have time and time again raped, beaten, mutilated, and killed the black woman for hundreds of years yet turn around and secretly place her above every other woman in the country. Their hope is that the rest of the world don't see it. The black woman, the epitome of grace and the roots of all hue-man beings. America created commemorative coins named Lady Liberty honoring women. The coins value was placed at one dollar. Until recently they decided to honor the black woman with the first 24-karat commemorative coin depicting her and her likeness and placed the value at one hundred dollars. The highest value placed on a woman's version of the commemorative coins. The black woman placed on the commemorative coin has the likeness of the original woman. She has full lips, naturally coiled hair braided and placed in a bun, a broad nose, and high cheek bones with a crown of stars on her head. She rests on the 225th anniversary lady liberty commemorative coin stamped with the years of 1792 – 2017. She is the first to be put on a 24-karat gold coin collection as an ethnic woman. There will be other women to follow but the black woman is the first. There is a far deeper meaning to her placement because she is the first woman to grace this planet period. In her secret honoring is a public one for the awakened black woman.

Now with that being said America has placed a value on her that supersedes that of others yet their value of the black woman is meaningless compared to the value that God has placed on her. In the realms of holiness, she is priceless no matter the value they place on her head.

She is the backbone of this world where the elixir of the God's flows from her womb and breasts. Her body is the instrument of holiness and bears the portal to the third realm. She is a creator and a healer but there's a negative side to the black woman when hurt and betrayal are placed upon her, she becomes cold and calculating. She shuts down in order to preserve what little dignity she has left. She starts to operate on auto pilot trying to make it from one moment to the next because day to day is too far away. She inwardly yearns for the love that she so rightfully deserves without knowing that it is already within her.

She struggles to over-stand the predicament she's in because of her choices and often wishes she could have done better.

The black woman on her quest to self has on more than one occasion misrepresented herself by not knowing who she truly is. She has thought of herself as less than and because of this behaved in a manner not befitting of a God.

She has fallen into the trap set by the other's and fed into the lies about her true identity. She has been casted out and traumatized repeatedly only to end up back on her feet. The black woman in all of her diversities can't and will not be kept down. She rises out of the ashes with the purity of that 24-karat gold.

The fire didn't take away from her spiritual beauty but added to it. The trauma that she has gone through has left her changed but not chained. The shackles that use to hang around her ankles have been broken off and the noose has been removed yet the psychological bondage still remains. She's been bound by her brain.

This type of bondage has her hindered in all areas of her life. She doesn't realize that the only one that has the ability to break her free from her bondage is her. In her unawakened state, she is waiting on someone else to do what only she can do.

The black woman with all of her scars still is searching although she isn't sure for what at this point in her journey, she just knows that something better is out there somewhere for her.

In all of this the black woman must be aware of people who are always telling her that God's time is the best when they are the ones holding up her progress. In their refusal to do their part. Remember time waits for no one. You must do what's required and that must start now.

Even in her current state she still yearns for the touch of a man but unfortunately for her once touched she realizes that it's not the touch that was required and it left her feeling void, empty, regretful, yearning, and lonely. His touch didn't fulfill the need that she had nor the desire. She wants her man and now knows that not any man can do what she needs to be done. That touch that she yearns for can only come from her Divine partner, that spirit made flesh. The one that she dreams of and yearns for but for now she settles for that temporary touch that just is not enough.

In her quest, she has become prey to the predator because they see the gift in her although she tries desperately to hide it. She pretends again to be just like everyone else and to no avail she fails.

The black woman with everything that she goes through still thinks of him and wonders where he is and what he's doing and why he's not by her side. She worries and wonders how much longer will it be before he figures out where he needs to be.

In her impatience, she settled and gave herself to another man, bore him children, and diverted from the Divine's plan only to find herself still yearning for the one that was created solely for her and her for him, now filled with guilt, shame, and regret, she looks at her life and what's left in horror because he's still in her heart and won't let go. That spirit turned flesh that just so happens to be the source of her unhappiness.

Everything that she does has become just routine, pretending by just letting things be but that nagging feeling just won't let her be. He's still there, etched in her spirit, molded to her DNA, designed in her fabric. The other part of her being.

She knows that he is getting close to finding her but the seconds seem like minutes and the minutes seem like hours and the hours seem like days and the days seem like weeks, and the weeks seem like months and the months seem like years and the years seem like an eternity. She has been waiting in the arms of another man who wasn't a part of the Divine's plan for her life. So, every night when he tries to hold her tight she cringes and pretends like everything's alright however she knows deep within that she will forever belong to another.

She has broken her own heart by not doing what's required and mistakenly over exaggerated her place in the wrong man's life. She now has babies by a man that she couldn't give her heart too and now her wounds have become scars that she has passed on to her children. They see the sadness in her eyes while she sings them sweet lullabies and taste the salt from the tears that caresses her face as she holds them in her embrace. The black woman filled with sadness as she tries to make sense of her madness.

Every day she awakens with the hope that this will be the day only to have her hopes dashed at dusk because he still hasn't found her. She goes to bed and hopes that he comforts her in her dreams where her lips will receive his kiss, her eyes feel his miss, her hands fill his caress, and her yoni his finesse. The black woman awakens again to tears, fears, and a never-ending desire to hear her man say, "I've come for you my dear."

The black woman has sent out all sorts of signals alerting the other part of herself that she is ready and willing to do what is required to complete the task only to continuously have her hopes yet again dashed. How much longer she keeps saying. Then she looks at the man that was meant to feel the space and decides that she will let go of the hopes of the other one and embrace what she has. So, she lovingly gives in and accepts her stand in and procreates with him yet again only to pretend to see her Divine partner's face and feel his embrace and wish she was in his space.

Now somewhere in the same time but different space there's a black man praying and hoping for the same black woman that's craving his embrace. He yearns for his Divine partner and doesn't know where she may be but he keeps looking.

In his quest to find his Divine he too strays entering one black hole after the other hoping that the next one will be hers but to no avail he keeps failing and falling short every time. He can't figure out what his problem is because each woman he finds is fine but they still don't have what he needs. He wants to love them but he can't because they are not her. He wants to give up the search and just settle for that one that comes close. So, he marries her and impregnates her only to end up day to day dreading her and his inability to find his Divine. He cries and tries just to come up short every time. He looks at the woman that he has settled for and enters her from behind hoping that if he pretends that she's her that he can ejaculate again this time. He has gotten good at pretending especially when he looks at his seeds manifested into flesh as the regret lingers in his mind like the smell of raw sex.

He manifests in his mind that he will try again just one more time, then goes on the hunt in search of his Divine. He analyzes every face and horns in on every smell as he begins to feel like hell. He knows that he has failed yet again to find his Divine. So, he settles for a one-night stand to quiet his screams from within.

"Just cum and go my friend," is the thought from within. So, he obliges and wastes his God's serum on another who it wasn't intended for, just to fill empty and depleted all over again. It wasn't worth it and he now feels shame and disappointment crying from his spirit again. A God behaving like an ordinary man can't take this foolishness again. He's being driven and misled by his sex organ and his head while denying what his heart has said. The black man. What a shame that the spirit being has to endure this painful experience as a hue-man being.

He lashes out in his pain hoping to hold on somehow and maintain the fake life that he's built trying to remain strong yet again, when inside he's dying from the pain of not having the other part of him. He smells her even though she's not near. He tastes her in every one of his tears. He feels her when he caresses himself. He sees her when he closes his eyes. He hears her when he's quietly alone on the road side. He the black man feels so lost, alone, and ashamed wondering what will she think, feel, and say on that day. He knows that his heart won't let him stay in this state of disarray and his spirit will push him again to seek his one and only true love and best friend, his Divine split from his within.

The black man is looked at as uncaring, unfazed, unbothered, doggish, and only wanting to get laid but is in spirit far removed from all of those things. He is loving, caring, bothered, fazed, in pain, trapped in his own maze. He wants desperately to be loved by her, his Divine that is. He needs her to filter him. He wants her to show him how to truly live from within. He needs to rest his head in her lap. He needs to weep on her shoulders. He needs to hear her thoughts so that he can merge them with his. He needs to spill his seed in her portal to be transformed into Gods kin. He needs her to take away all the troubles of this world as he lays in her arms being soothe like that of a newborn just entering this realm. He needs her and not any other.

The black man hurts like no other because of his fear of having to be with another and dreading having to pretend to be strong as he wrestles with his spirit from within. He knows in his heart he can't win operating in the flesh, while secretly wishing he could operate from total spiritual-ness. The black man caught in all his mess has settled and now married to his regrets as he tries desperately to find a way out of his mess. He yearns for her and she yearns for him. They both secretly yearn for them. The them that they were created to be. The them that now lives in pain, regret, and misery. The them that were created for one another who has on their quest vowed to be forever infused with one another. The them that struggles from day to day. The them that wants to erase the current time and travel back to that happy place. The place where they laughed, caressed, kissed, and touched one another's face. The time when all was well and life was filled with the air of the God's. Where there were no assignments, no need to leave their place of holiness. A place where love reigned supreme and there was no negative energy and no demonic beings. A place filled with the energy of the God's and all things pure came straight from the heart. A place where death didn't exist. A place of sheer wonder and pure bliss. A place nothing like this.

The black man and the black woman separated by hue-man-ness yet together by spiritual-ness while yearning for true oneness.

« CHAPTER 27 PHYSICAL EXTERNAL »

The black man has been tricked by the others into thinking that he needs more than one woman because there's a shortage of men and that, he deserves it, right, wrong.

The others know that when they get the black man to think this they have taken over his mind and when the black man acts upon this they have then taken over his heart, the purest part of himself where the God in him resides.

They know that the true purpose of the black man is to fuse to the black woman, the only woman that he was designed for and by design the only one that can truly transform him because she is the other part of him.

The others also know that this can't happen if the black man is in conflict, confusion, and division with more than one woman at the same time. The black man can only be filtered by one woman, period! He was not designed to have more than one woman to pull from him. However, in his foolish thinking he thinks that he is a stud for spilling his seed into more than one and rightfully so because again this is what the slave master trained him to do, BREED!

The black man was stripped of his knowing of self and taught to breed with as many women as possible then leave. He was turned into the lowest form of an animal. Taught to devoid and detach himself from any and all things sacred and holy, the black woman.

The black man has been so badly damaged that he doesn't even see himself as damaged. He thinks his ways have always been such. Falling into the myth that there is a shortage of men so he needs to fill in the gap by having as many women as possible even going so far as to marry more than one woman to help the cause all in the name of religion of course.

He has been fooled by the others and now he is fooling himself by refusing to awaken from his slumber and do what's required to fix his mess. He refuses to take ownership of his part in this chaotic mess that he's in. It doesn't matter what his social, economic, nor financial standing, he's still sleeping.

Polygamy is one of the greatest atrocities brought about in the black man's sleeping state. The dividing of himself in the name of **procreational duties**. He thinks that he has a right to leave behind as many children as possible and that this and having multiple women somehow makes him a MAN, yeah right. No, really, right. In this society set by the others it does make him their definition of a man. This is clear cut designing on the part of the others, masterful even. The others have mastered the part of convincing the black people that they aren't relevant.

The black man in this state is the lack man and this man of lack has refused to take back what's rightfully his. He lacks in all areas because he keeps trying to be something that he's not. Patterning himself after something that is of lesser quality and value than himself by not being totally aware of who he is as the original man cut from the cloth of the Gods, molded and groomed to rule beside the black woman.

One would wonder just how did the black woman and the black man end up in this predicament in the first place. Well it's actually simple, they created it. When they entered into this realm and decided to delay the assignment given to them, they created chaos. This chaos gave birth to indecisiveness and this indecisiveness gave birth to the loop hole that allowed Godliness to turn into Royalty and Royalty to turn into peasantry and peasantry to turn into slavery. The black woman and the black man have created a firestorm of mass destruction on themselves during this moment of chaos.

While they weren't paying attention, the others were and this allowed the others to infiltrate an already damaged system. Once the infiltration was successful the others then studied the black woman and the black man. During this studying process, they learned from the black woman and the black man how to treat and take over them, and they did.

The others played the black woman and the black man against one another. It was a simple strategy yet ingenious. The others took an already fragile situation and turn it critical. Now all these years later the black woman and the black man are still in this critical state of being.

Outwardly they sometimes appear to be gaining some of their territory back but inwardly they haven't moved an inch. When they do start awakening they start to remember their royal heritage and then start to battle one another on which part of that royal heritage is true when in fact that is another trick of the others to stop the black woman and the black man from moving further in the awakening process. The others don't want the black woman and the black man to get to the point of total awakening. Total awakening is when they remember their space before time, when they remember that they in fact are more than mere royalty, when they remember that they are GODS!

The others have developed clever distractions to constantly keep the black woman and the black man busy fighting meaningless causes that have nothing and I mean absolutely nothing to do with them. These causes aren't even causes they are carefully placed deterrence's.

As long as you are fighting about who was in Kemet and when or who was the first Moor's and why, you will get nowhere on this journey. This journey is far deeper than Kemet and Moor's. It's about you remembering where you were before you came to this planet and who you were. You must learn to dig deeper than the surface to get to the roots of who you are. There is no greater discovery than that of self.

You have a duty to yourself and that includes you doing what is required for you! What brings you happiness should be top priority. If it's seeing a certain face or hearing a certain voice then make sure that face and voice are a part of your life no matter what. Surround yourself with irreplaceable people that have the same flow as you do. The ones that assist you in your growing process and not those that are just around for monetary means.

Loyalty is a gift and whosoever is in your mist and are loyal, you better make sure you are the same because loyalty and love go hand and hand. And is not as common as one would have you think.

Make sure while you are pressing forward in your journey that you don't mistreat those that are loyal and loving towards you in the name of progress because you don't know who you might need later on. Rest assured that when you have true loyalty and mistreat it, you will not come across it so easily again and may just have to go back to the place you found it from at first.

The pursuit is for love and with love comes an abundance of other positive things. No one is the primary source of your happiness but the one for you will surely add to it. They will compliment you as both a spiritual and a physical being. They will stretch you and challenge you to be a better being. They will not just simply tell you something because you want to hear it. Their truth to you may initially sting but later on you will appreciate the honesty they bring because it is beneficial to your cause.

Every decision you make should be always made out of love and the first love is the love of self and when you are operating out of love of self you will also be operating in love of the ones who love you. Love has a magnet effect. It will draw to it what it already is. So, when you start operating within the confines of love you then become surrounded by love. Love is an elixir for all that ails you on this planet and when you are filled with love it automatically releases itself to those who need it. Once you release your power of love onto those that need it they will forever be a part of your fabric no matter what. They become a part of you on all levels and when you least expect it they will need more. Love is external and internal. Love is physical and spiritual. Love is the highest form of praise. Love is Godly and Godliness is Love.

It is the reason for you being here on this planet. So, find a way to keep searching for the love that you came to this world for and if you have already found that love then make sure you do what is required to keep it because contrary to what others may have told you love doesn't just die on its own, you kill love with your mistreatment of it.

Don't take love for granted thinking it will always be there, even love doesn't want to be treated badly. Love is not painful nor is love ignorant. Love just wants what it already is and that's love, so in essence love wants itself, the other part of itself and will keep searching until it finds it.

The love of a conscious black woman is deep because it penetrates all layers of the fabric of who you are. She touches your spirit. Her kisses send electric currents throughout your body. Her yoni is different from the others because the conscious black woman's yoni is a place of rest for the awakening black man. She builds him, comforts him, lays him in her lap and soothes his torment.

She is who he is and he is who she is. They are them and they are they. They are Gods. Drawn to one another like the magnets that they are. The magnetic forces that drew them together are the same forces that created them. The creators of all things relevant and majestic. The eyes of essence and the lovers of love.

The conscious black man wants the conscious black woman that he was created for and when he finds her nothing can stop him from gaining what rightfully belongs to him. No matter the circumstance he will find a way to complete his mission. When a conscious black man feels that first spark of familiarity from his conscious black woman his initial response is fear. This fear is felt due to shock. He is shocked that he finally found his her. The her that was created for him but once that fear subsides its full speed ahead. He will be like a full throttled locomotive and nothing and no one can stop him.

This is the turning point for him and he has waited a lifetime to get here and due to his initial fear, he may stumble in the beginning. The conscious black woman is aware of this dilemma and will even warn him because she has stepped into consciousness before him. This may cause a delay in their quest because he feels threatened by her strength and spiritual abilities.

The conscious black woman will go through periods of loneliness when the half awakened black man backslides. This loneliness is the fault of the black man and he knows it but because he has one foot on the conscious side of the fence and the other foot on the unconscious side of the fence, he dangles in between his will to do what is required and his will of doing his best and if not careful, he will choose his best and temporarily loose the conscious black woman. With love your best is never enough because your best is hue-manly and not spiritual.

When the conscious black woman and the conscious black man start to feel one another spiritually their love draws them to one another and the closer they become the stronger the love is. The strength of that love creates a bond that no other force can break.

That love makes everything different than before. They see things in unison. They hear things in unison. They feel things in unison. She knows her man like no other and he knows his woman like no other. When they're apart time nor distance can separate the two because they have been fused together spiritually in a way that the natural mind can't comprehend. Even strangers can feel the energetic force that connects the two. There is an aura that surrounds them and when they touch it is Angelical, it is Godly.

When the conscious black man enters his conscious black woman, he knows that afterwards he will never be the same. Her touch sends shockwaves throughout his entire body and it's not like anything that he has ever felt before. He loses the hue-man part of himself in her and finds the spirit part of himself within her. He transforms within the confines of her dark hole; her heavenly portal takes him to places naturally unknown but spiritually so familiar.

The conscious black man takes his time as he navigates through her moist terrain. He meticulously handles her with great ease as he should because she is his entry way to the places beyond this space and time. The conscious black man doing all that he can to ensure that nothing happens to his conscious black woman. Created for he and she for him he buries himself deeper into the folds of her miraculous treasure and never let's go. He has branded her, put his seal on the inside of their private space. He has marked his territory as occupied and dares anyone who tries to enter for a ride. He knows the value of what he has as time has taught him that there is no other like her and if he is to get to where he needs to be spiritually he must continue to fuse, bond, mold, and never let go of the one who was created especially for him.

There are moments when the conscious black man slips back into his sleeping state and starts to feel unworthy of the love that she has for him and those are the times where the conscious black woman must ask him to let her love him. She asks for permission to ensure that he is ready again to receive the power that she has to give to him because if she gives him the power when he is not ready it will kill him literally. He has to want what she has or it will be the cause of his demise. The power that the conscious black woman possesses is not of this world, it is of a place and space like no other and once she has tapped into that source she is a force to be reckoned with. She can build up and tear down. She can create whatever she wants when given the right elements to work with.

Anyone and everyone in the pathway of the conscious black woman will be blessed just by being in her presence alone. Her life force is so powerful that even her enemies want to be a part of it. She is and will always be the strongest and most powerful force in the lives of everyone she comes in contact with. They will never forget her because she has left fragments of the holiness she has with them.

« CHAPTER 28 PHYSICAL INTERNAL »

There is no greater love than the love of self and by self, I mean both parts of you spiritually. The inner you moves from glory to glory on a quest for true Divine happiness while on this planet and when it is achieved you as a natural hue-man being transform. Your walk and talk changes because you are filled with the Holy of the Holy by design and crave it by choice. You now want what your spirit wants.

The battle lines have been drawn and that negative aura must bow and be put in its place. You know that a battle has ensued but you also know beforehand who the winner is. You know that long before a battle starts that training must take place. You know you can't wait until time to step on the battle field before you start preparing for the fight.

Your training and preparations started long before you became aware of the need to fight. This fight began long before you entered into this realm and it started as a spiritual fight then turned into a physical and a spiritual one once you entered this planet.

You knew nothing but love and holiness and then a part of yourself was removed and sent away from you and you started to feel things that you never felt before and it didn't feel good. You learned quickly what pain was and it hurt really bad. You didn't like the feeling of pain and wanted quickly to relieve yourself of it but you didn't initially know how. So, you began to search for an answer and the answer came. You learned that your pain reliever was attached to the other part of yourself that part that had been removed from you and you needed to quickly find it. You then began to search for where to look and found out where but not exactly where just a regional area. So, you said "okay that's close enough" and you went looking and searching for you.

The journey wasn't as easy as you initially thought. It hurt bad to find this out too. The region you thought was small ended up being far bigger than it seemed. You now roam from place to place searching and every time you get close something shifts and you're back at square one again.

Love being the key component in your quest keeps you moving even when you decide to give up, it is love that won't let you. The force that pushes you pass your insecurities and doubts, that makes you smile when you think of the outcome in the mist of the current storm, it is love.

No matter the current circumstances you must stay focused on the outcome. Tunnel vision is what is needed at this point in your quest. Tunnel vision is when you by choice only see what's ahead and what's ahead of you is her, your finish line. There is nothing outside of you more important than her because she is the prize, the quest is for her. It doesn't matter what's on the sidelines or who has been a side chick, this my dear is about her and you. Your conscious black woman, your destination, your revelation, your moral compass, your filter, your love.

No one and I mean no one can take her place because there is none like her. She is the be in your being and you know it and so does she. She pushes and pulls you. She molds and grooms you. She relishes and relates to you. She maneuvers and masters you because in doing so she knows that she is doing so for herself. You are her and she is you. Remember again YOU are HER and SHE is YOU!

You both are connected spiritually and must work as a unit and have the ultimate goal of oneness in focus. To be fused, soldered, pulled into one another so deep that even you can't tell the difference because there is no longer two. The two has joined and became the ultimate one. One. One. One. Oneness.

You should by now be thinking everything as one. She is the one when you pull into her and you are the one when she allows you to pull into her because you are gaining entry into the source of power that you and her live for. It is this source that makes you one. It is this source that heals and protects the both of you and it must be utilized daily because it is food and medicine for the nourishment of the body, mind, and spirit. The more you enter the better you feel for her and you. Your goal is to work your way up until you are entering her portal more than once a day. Its nourishment remember and even with your physical food you eat more than once a day. There is no need to fast from her because this will cause a breakdown in all realms and a disconnect. You must constantly replenish yourself so you won't leave any gaps and openings for the negative forces to get through. They can only infiltrate you when you have gone without nourishment from your Divine portal. Depending on the circumstances you may need to enter her on the spur of the moment. An unexpected shift in the atmosphere will cause this to be needed immediately. She will know this and quickly oblige you because she is fully aware.

The conscious black woman that you have is always watching and paying attention to everything that concerns you because she knows that you may leave room for error, you are her and she is you. When she spots a change in your demeanor along with a shift in the universe she will quickly come to your aid before you are even aware of the need to be revitalized. This woman that you have is none like no other and as you continue on the journey with her you will constantly see that. Her evolution is amazing in itself and for you to see it in motion is miraculous to say the least.

The conscious black woman rides the waves of despair like the God that she is and conquers things that mere mortals can't even fathom. She in her Godliness is in awe of herself because she knows and overstands that nothing she does is because of her flesh but all because of her spirit. She bows even to the spiritual part of herself because she knows that her love of the inner her is the love of the outer her and the love of the outer her is the love of the ultimate her. She knows. She knows. She knows.

This is the part that confuses the unconscious black woman and the unconscious black man because they can't seem to get just how the conscious black woman does what she does and makes it look so effortlessly. It is all in part due to the Divine order placed on the life that she lives. She is protected by the Supreme being and no matter how much pain and trauma she has had to undergo on this planet nothing can remove the hands of God from her life.

She must do what is required of her no matter what anyone thinks or says because her journey is never about them and she knows that. This is why she holds her head high as she walks through the storms that being on this planet brings and doesn't take for granted what has been gifted to her because she knows not everyone gets that.

When she takes a stand nothing and no one can make her sit down. Her tenacity is a driving force. She is a builder, leader, conqueror, and teacher to her conscious black man. She is a raging storm when threatened by anyone who dares to challenge the pathway to her mission and her man is off limits to everyone that brings negativity their way.

The conscious black woman knows that the only boundaries placed on her are those that she inadvertently placed on herself because no one on this planet has that kind of power over her. She is boundless in the spirit and the only boundaries that are there are the ones that she uses to keep the others at bay.

She is the ultimate protector and will cut out anyone and anything that threatens the safety and sanctity of her union with her man.

She is gentle with him and ferocious when she has to be towards others. She knows that her man is strong but with her in his arms he is gentle and meek. He humbles himself at her feet because he knows that she is the source of everything that he is on this planet. She shivers at the thought of his touch and he elongates at the thought of hers. Even when they are physically apart they are spiritually together. One on one. Joined at the request of the Gods, moved from glory to glory. Writing every word of their story. Humbled, elegant, transparent to one another.

Agile when it comes to their cause from beginning to beginning with no ending in sight. Oneness transformed with everyday a new beginning to all that they are and all that they hope to be. Every time he pulls into her it is new, a first time experience every single time. They are virgins to one another over and over again and this makes their love stronger because they know that every moment plugged into her is new.

Amazed at the feelings that's so hard for them to explain because no words are apparent in the throes of their passionate love making. The making of love is new every time because they are new every time. It is powerful. It is harmonious. It is sacred. It is holy. The thought of it sends shivers down their spines. The anticipation moves them to complete whatever they have to do so that they can join again. Charging their bodies in preparation for the tasks that they must complete so that they can join again and again and again. Repeating the pull in process as often as possible. They know that everything leads back to them and everything starts with them and the more they utilize one another the more effective they become which requires them to pull into one another more often.

Creating the bond that is required to get them what they need. Taking ownership of one another as they fuse and mold their togetherness. She owns him and he owns her, their spirits merging and becoming one every time they bond. Bonding moment to moment. Tightened by the pull in process. Recharged by the moment of conquest. Shared in the evidence of all things unseen. Foretold of the making of everything seen. Leaning and relying on one another for all things them.

The conscious black man loves his conscious black woman with every fiber of his being and doesn't care who knows it because he knows in loving her he is loving himself. Being in love is operating in the will of love itself. It is being on the inside of it and it on the inside of you. Being in love is deeper than loving because loving although still a spiritual act is not the highest order. However, being in love is putting yourself on the inside of the core experience, you become fused with it, you become it. You become love and love becomes you. Being in love becomes a continuous act of Godliness. It becomes the height of praise and worship. It is acceptance. It is abundance. It is you.

Your journey is moved ahead with excitement and joy knowing that love flows within you. You are in love and love is in you.

Being in love offers a craving of itself and the craving of love is the most intense feeling you will ever have and you will do whatever is required to fulfill that craving. I am not speaking of a lustful craving because that type of craving is not Godly. Godly cravings of being in love comes from the root core of you and once you step in love you want to stay in love. You want to have love in you at all times. The thought of being in love moves you into glorious oneness.

Being in love, the seen and the unseen of glories. The height of your life as a hue-man and spirit being.

Most people on this planet will never experience this type of love because they aren't capable of receiving it. This type of love has a strength that will kill you if you received it and it wasn't meant for you. This type of love is reserved for the one that it is intended for and nothing and no one can change that. This type of love makes your heart skip a beat and weep while yearning for it. This type of love needs to be needed and wants to be wanted by the other part of itself. This type of love is only gifted to the one that it was created for. This type of love. This type of love. This type of love has the ability to stop all things hurtful. It feels so good when you are in it and it feels so good when it is in you.

Love doesn't hurt, nor harm, nor maim, nor pain you. Love heals, builds, and cures. Love, the epitome of all things Godly. Love waits for itself to be received by the one it was created for. Love makes the crooked roads straight and the narrow roads wide.

Love is growth and blissfulness, honorable, respectful, and justifiable. Love opens you up to receive it when you want and need it. It changes your outlook on everything. Love wants to be loved in return. Love weeps tears of joy at the mere thought of being reciprocated as the magnetic effect draws love closer to itself.

The fulfillment of everything continues on the rightful pathway of love. Strengthen in unison and reciprocated in holiness. Love, the essence of gracefulness. Joined at the roots by faithfulness.

Don't fall in love as if it were some accident waiting to happen. Honor love by making the conscious choice to put yourself into it, by being in love with both parts of yourself. The him and her parts of you. Love is instantaneous. It doesn't require time it only requires you to be consciously aware of it. Now awaken and be in love.

Love the foundation by which all things must be based upon. It is the root of all things Godly and nothing can separate you from the power of Love not even hate. Hatred is the byproduct of the lack of real love in your life. Without real love, nothing you do will bring about the true manifestation of God's ultimate blessing which is complete oneness. You will be forever aimlessly wondering about on this planet seeking material things and missing the true wonders of love and what it brings. Hate is a dis-ease of the body, mind, and Spirit whereas Love is the comfort and ease of all facets of you. Love is to be consciously aimed for and always the main goal in this pursuit of life.

Love needs no explanation, only clear and precise communication.

« CHAPTER 29 EXTERNAL SPIRIT »

There's a life force far stronger than you can ever imagine and greater. There are also things that dwell with us that we oftentimes can't see but all the time feel. Yet we dismiss it and try to rationalize it. That presence that you feel is real and has been with you before time existed. Some call them Guardian Angels, some say the Holy Spirit. I will just call them Divine, the Holy of the Holy.

The spirits assigned to watch over and shield you when you aren't aware and able to protect yourself especially during the sleeping phase of your life.

Often people generally take for granted the fact that everyone deals with pain and suffering differently and what one may be able to handle may literally kill the next person.

Those that are the weakest requires the most assistance and it may not seem fair to those that are the strongest because pain is pain no matter who bears it. Although some may think that just because another person is stronger that you can just keep piling pain after pain on them like their pain don't hurt and that they can't break.

It's like polygamy and the idea that it is acceptable for a man to have more than one wife or woman that he is having sex with in the same house with him. This type of thinking is nothing but grandeur and those who participate in this type of an arrangement aren't doing so for the sake of love but rather for the sake of lust and loss. They aren't even aware of the spiritual implications of this act alone. Some even try to rationalize it by saying "Oh, they did it in Africa." They think that this journey on this planet is about culture and tradition when it is far deeper than that. No man can spiritually nor sexually successfully take care of more than one conscious black woman. It is not possible because of who she is.

Now in the natural the others have forced the black man and the black woman to breed for monetary gain and thus causing a situation that has rendered both the black woman and the black man useless in certain areas when it comes to intimacy and sex. When I speak of the natural I am speaking of the unawakened black woman and the unawakened black man.

If polygamy was what is considered natural then you wouldn't have division and envy in the homes. The strife that draws a wedge would be none existent.

Hue-man beings do things that are hurtful to one another because of the lack of love they have for self and when they realize what they have done it's usually too late to fix it. Most unconscious black women share a man because they feel like they don't have any other options. The esteem of things have failed them and they feel the need to join with someone even when they know that it will bring them misery. Just for the sake of saving face they pretend like all is well and they like it.

Scars from past trauma leaves the unawakened at a disadvantage because of the things that they have had to endure. The pain they try to cope with hinders their ability to see things from a positive prospective and because of this they sometimes can't make the right decisions that's most beneficial for them.

They deny themselves the essential things necessary for their development and refuse to allow the spirits to assist them. The force that lingers right at the vocal cords they won't even utilize because of the fear that they have for succeeding. Yes, you read it right. They have an overwhelming fear of success. They have become bunk mates with pain and despair and pain free and success frightens them. They sabotage their progress because failure has become familiar. It is this familiarity that keeps them company on the nights when they are alone and soaking their pillows with tears of sadness and disappointment. They are afraid of the unknown so they stick with what they known even though it hurts.

There is a saying amongst some that says, "the devil you know is better than the angel you don't know." This is the type of thinking that hinders you on all levels. For one it is not true and two it is teaching you to sub-consciously stay in a bad situation because it is familiar. Look, familiar doesn't equate to right or healthy or good. Refusing to leave a situation just because you have been in it for a long time doesn't mean that you are a failure. If you wake up and see that it hurts then by all means do what is required to remove yourself from the hurtful situation. It may not be simple but it is a must.

You have to learn to love yourself in a way that gives you the strength to do what is required for you.

There will be moments when you will feel down and wonder what are you really doing as you bear the pain from the scars. You question the choices you made as you navigate in your mind through all of the trauma that has happened to you. Your time in this life may seem like it has been in vain as you struggle to keep everything afloat. Just know that nothing in this lifetime can stop you from achieving what you came here to achieve. Your age, your size, financial status, marital status, nor family background can hinder your progress as long as you keep doing what's required.

There is only one thing stopping you from doing what is required and that's your fear. You are afraid to step into your purpose. That fear has you in a false state of paralysis. To you it appears that you aren't moving because the fear blinds you from seeing the baby steps that you have taken. The fear hinders you from seeing that you have already made it through your worst of times and what's ahead of you is the best of times. Your life is about to take a drastic turn, for the better. Just keep forging ahead and you will see the fruits of your labor. Everything that you went through was to guide you closer to your Divine purpose. The pain and agony was warranted because of who you are. That pain and agony pushed you pass your fears right into your promise. You used that hurt and anger to catapult yourself right where you needed to be. For every set back was a comeback. Yes, it hurt and yes it still hurts but look at the outcome.

Look at yourself and all that you have gone through. Now look at yourself again and all that you have accomplished in the mist of your pain and suffering. Now look at yourself one more time. See, you are the comeback. Stop being afraid to live the life that was intended for you. You deserve every good thing that is happening in your life right now. You paid the price to be where you are. It was your sweat, tears, and even blood that got you where you are.

Every time you feel like giving up and the road ahead seems bleak and cloudy just remember that you have made it through the bleak and cloudy days before and it didn't stop you from achieving. You may have been slowed down but you definitely wasn't stopped.

Take a moment if you need to, to cry and scream. Feel whatever emotion you need to feel just don't stay in the negative too long. The negative release is necessary because you can't keep that inside you and expect to get positive. Releasing moves out what's not needed and replaces it with what is needed. That's why it is not good to keep negative emotions pinned up inside of you. This pinned up negativity causes disease physically, psychologically, and spiritually. You must release it within a healthy time frame.

Now once your time of negative release is over then you must refuel yourself with positive energy. You do this by loving. Yes, loving yourself. Forgive yourself for making the miss-takes because it is those mistakes that allowed you to see what you didn't need nor want in your life. Also keep in mind that everything that's negative weighs you down and everything that's positive lifts you up. The lifting up of oneself keeps you in a state of elevation which enables you to maintain a better view of the things and people around you and to see yourself and them through fresh eyes, even a renewed awareness.

The key to moving forward is to embrace every facet of yourself and allow yourself the necessary time to heal from the damage that you caused yourself. Learn to embrace the being that you are and accept you for being you.

« CHAPTER 30 INTERNAL SPIRIT »

The conscious black woman and the conscious black man are Gods and kindreds to the Sun which flows through their bodies as liquid melanin.

Melanin. Kissed by the Sun and caressed by the Moon and created by the Gods to rule and reign, to govern and gain, to watch and maintain one another.

Melanin gifted to the black woman and the black man from the Gods that chose this form of blessing so that all that sees and knows, they are the chosen ones. The ones that never have to believe that they are the ones but to look at the melanated skin and see just who they are and how blessed they are because of being the chosen ones. Melanated and originated from the

Holy of Holy and chosen and used as the standard by which all others will be copied. Seldom imitated but never duplicated. The black man and the black woman have been harvested for their body parts because of who they are and who they represent. Their organs are far more superior than any other people on this planet and this is one of the reasons why so many black people are deemed missing around the world, when in all actuality they aren't missing they have been taken. Yes, taken. Taken for the gifts they have in their possession.

Every part of the black hue-man beings hold a holy significance that the others do not possess and they know this and for this reason they are fearful of the black woman and the black man. Fearful because they do not overstand how and why the black people were chosen instead of them to possess such sacredness.

The sad reality to all of this is the unconscious black woman and the unconscious black man pose no threat to the others. It is only the conscious black woman and the conscious black man that threaten the livelihood of the others because they know who they are and their purpose for being in this realm. They do not bow and they do not break at the falsehood of rulership that the others possess.

The unconscious black woman and the unconscious black man have fallen into the trap of thinking that they are inferior when in fact they are not, even in the unconscious state. The unawakened black woman and the unawakened black man in their sleeping state still possess a holiness that the others will never have. The gift is still the gift even when it's still wrapped. Just because you haven't opened the gift yet doesn't mean that it's not still in your possession.

The unconscious black woman and the unconscious black man are constantly sent signals from their spirit but don't recognized the signals because of their unconscious state however they are still aware that something is off. They sense that something somewhere is not right and what they are doing to themselves is wrong. That gut feeling, they get that won't go away when they partake in certain things is the greatest indicator. No one has to tell them because it is apparent. This is also the reason for many of the storms that rise up in their lives. But are they aware that all the storms in their lives have a purpose?

The purpose for each and every storm when it looms in your life is to get your attention, to make you think, and to make you do what is required to move you into position to be abundantly blessed in the area of anointing.

Every time you pray and ask God to do something or give something there is a shift in the universe on your behalf. Once the universe moves for you, you have to move for the universe but if you don't do your part then a storm rises. The storm comes because you aren't in the position that you need to be to receive what you asked for. So, the storm comes and forces you to move into the correct position and depending on your ability to comprehend what's happening at that time you may have a short storm or a long one or a mild one or a strong one. You determine the length and severity of your storm by your initial response. It is and has always been your response to the events in your life that either make or breaks you. You are the key component in all of this because it is your life, your legacy, your love.

The scars bear no significance to you being who you are because that was determined before you entered into this realm. You are you no matter what happens. Whether conscious or unconscious. However, the power you possess is only effective when you know how to use it and this you must learn how to do.

You may not have a physical teacher but don't use this as an excuse for lack of trying because you can always call upon your spirit for assistance and your spirit will gladly oblige you.

Everything happens when you are ready for it to happen and if what you have been praying for hasn't manifested in this realm it is because you didn't do what was required. So, in essence you weren't ready.

Preparations must be made for every request you make to the Divine. Surely you don't expect to get anything from the Holy of Holy without having to do anything for it. You have to go through the process of preparation to receive. Now once you have completed the preparation part then you go into the next phase of the blessing process. Your request to receive is duly noted by God and taken into careful consideration. Yes, it is Divinely analyzed and depending on the analysis you may or may not receive a yes but no matter what you will get an answer. Just over-stand that some prayers are answered no and the no is because you are not ready to receive the yes.

There are times in your life when you think you want something when in all actuality your reasons for wanting it aren't genuine nor pure.

Here's an example that you can relate to. School is about to start back after the summer vacation. You know that during the summer you have to get certain things before school starts because the supplies you had the previous year have all been used and you've outgrown your previous clothes. Okay now you don't wait until the first day of school to scrabble around to every all-night store to start purchasing the items needed. This is the same way with preparing for your prayers to be answered. You must get ready and stay ready.

Whatever it is that you are asking the universe for get ready to receive that yes. Yes! Act like you already have the yes. You'll have what you want when you do what's required.

From this day forward in the mist of the storm prepare for what is to come when the storm is over. Life must go on and nothing and no one should be allowed to stop your preparation process because no matter what and who you have to live beyond the storms in your life.

When preparing remember to prepare in love, for love, and with love. Love will allow you to see and feel everything from God's prospective instead of your hue-manly one.

No matter what happens or is happening right now count your blessings and remember that you must be willing to do what's required to receive what you've asked for. The bigger the request the more preparations you have to make. You have the power, now use it.

You are free to choose whatever you want, however make sure you are prepared for the consequences of your choices.

There is no greater moment on this planet than that of experiencing true love and when you do don't allow fear to stop you from being totally engulfed in what only God has gifted you with. It is God that transformed that fear into fortunate and allowed the spirit to lead me back to the very one that held my heart and the other portion of my spirit.

Love doesn't come with obstacles. However, people do and when a person is blessed enough to encounter true love they must do what is required to stay in it and to allow it to stay in you. It is unfortunate that the hue-man-ness will push you away from the very spiritualness that you need to continuously operate within the sanctity of true love because true love to a hue-man makes them appear to be vulnerable. True Love can be scary to the hue-man side of you and can cause you to run from the very Love that you require because of fear.

I had to learn that the hard way and I am thankful to God that my Divine's Love for me wouldn't let my heart go. His spirit held onto my spirit and embedded itself so deep within my core and nourished me from the inside out until I was ready to receive. Our spirits knew what our hue-man-ness didn't because we belong to one another. I am his and he is mine, through eternity and no matter how many lifetimes.

APPENDIX

Chapter 1 Abrasions, contains definition from Webster's dictionary.

Chapter 2 Bruised and Broken, contains definition from Webster's dictionary.

Chapter 3 Cuts, contains definitions from Webster's dictionary.

Chapter 4 Defaced by Deja Vu, contains definitions from Webster's dictionary.

Chapter 5 Erosions, contains definitions from Webster's dictionary.

Chapter 6 Fractures, contains definitions from Webster's dictionary.

Chapter 7 Gash, contains definitions from Webster's dictionary.

Chapter 8 Hemorrhage, contains definitions from Webster's dictionary.

Chapter 9 Incisions, contains definitions from Webster's dictionary.

Chapter 10 Jagged, contains definitions from Webster's dictionary.

Chapter 11 Keloids, contains definitions from Webster's dictionary.

Chapter 12 Lesions, contains definitions from Webster's dictionary.

Chapter 13 Maimed, contains definitions from Webster's dictionary.

Chapter 14 Nicks, contains definitions from Webster's dictionary.

Chapter 15 Opprobrium, contains definitions from Webster's dictionary.

Chapter 16 Puncture, contains definitions from Webster's dictionary.

Chapter 17 Questions.

Chapter 18 Remnant, contains definitions from Webster's dictionary.

Chapter 19 Scratch, contains definitions from Webster's dictionary.

Chapter 20 Tattoo, contains definitions from Webster's dictionary.

Chapter 21 Underlying, contains definitions from Webster's dictionary.

Chapter 22 Vitiate, contains definitions from Webster's dictionary.

Chapter 23 Wounded, contains definitions from Webster's dictionary.

Chapter 24 X Marks the Spot

Chapter 25 You.

Chapter 26 Zero in on Target contains information from U.S. government website.

Chapter 27 Physical External.

Chapter 28 Physical Internal.

Chapter 29 External Spirit
Chapter 30 Internal Spirit.

NOTES

We as SPIRIT beings have a responsibility to ourselves to forge ahead as the God's that we are.

We, the true HUE-MAN beings while on this planet have endured many hardships but we have also had many accomplishments as well. We have had our own communities, cities, and townships once upon a time. However, Black Wall Street and the many other accomplishments that we have had physically can never equate to the mass treasures that we have been gifted with spiritually.

Although material wealth is nice to have while on this planet because it allows for a more comfortable way of living while here, it is not the purpose of our quest to Divine Oneness.

We as a people, as diverse as we are, must learn that unity and love are the foundations by which we must maintain our rightful place on this planet. We are our greatest gifts to one another physically and the sharing of love is our greatest gift spiritually. Have you shared your gift of love today?

LINKS

www.amazon.com/victoriaamidou

www.barnesandnoble.com/victoriaamidou

www.facebook.com/victoriaamidoullc

www.iheartradio.com/victoriaamidou

www.instagram.com/victoriaamidou

www.itunes.com/victoriaamidou

www.twitter.com/victoriaamidou

www.youtube.com/victoriaamidou

Research and informational sources:

www.merriam-webster.com

www.usmint.gov

OVERVIEW

Healing does not mean that you come out without scars. There are some wounds that leave damaged tissue above and below the surface. You have healed, you're just not the same. A wound, even healed can still be the cause of great pain and agony, which on some days can be unbearable.

Some scars are so profound that they are a constant reminder of the trauma that you have experienced, so much so that even others can see and feel them. Some even wear their scars as a badge of honor while others wear them with shame.

No matter the cause of your scars just know that there is nothing that can stop you from achieving what has been chosen for you by the Divine.

It is your duty to yourself to take the necessary steps to ensure that you do what's required and that starts with learning to truly love yourself.

AUTHOR

Victoria Amidou is an Ordained Minister, Spiritual Counselor, Entrepreneur, International Lecturer, Life Coach, Inspirational Speaker, Keynote Speaker, Motivational Speaker, Speech Writer, Song Writer, Singer, Activist, Actress, Author, Voice-Over Artist and Poet.

Victoria Amidou presides as CEO of Victoria Amidou LLC, Victoria Amidou Ministries, Ministerial Research Services, and is an Ambassador for God.

Victoria Amidou is a passionate representative of The Most High God and has been chosen for such a path to empower those who are broken on a pathway to mending while using key principals in the Holy Word to counteract the damage that has been inflicted upon God's children.

Victoria Amidou travels the world teaching to those that are hungry for the knowledge of who God truly is and how to use the gifts already within to effectively heal and deal with the traumatic events that has them stuck, stagnant, and at a standstill in their lives.

Victoria Amidou began her quest to true deliverance when trauma struck her to a point of near death. The pain was so intense that she at the crossroads decided to completely surrender to God in a way that would change everything as she knew it. It was at that point when she started studying like never before and the subject was a difficult one, it was the study of self.

Victoria Amidou's quest took her to places of brokenness that she thought had mended. Through her self-examination she learned the true meaning of self-love and how to live the life that God intended for her to live.

Victoria Amidou learned the value of receiving and the value of pain and that nothing can stop her from her purpose but her.

Victoria Amidou has taken the shatter pieces and created a legacy of love that she is able to share with those who are willing to receive that which God has gifted to her.

POETRY

X MARKS THE SPOT

The exact spot in time where her lack of reason took over her mind seemed so far removed from this lifetime as she battled to remain sane in a place filled with insanity.

The scars that mark the spot create the perfect x at the round of her back all the way up to her neck from the iron she wore as a choke holding collar.

The black woman muffling her cries as she recalls the voice of her dead mother singing her praises and sweet lullabies during a time when royalty reigned and God's came to break bread and talk of a time before this one came.

Oh, what a shame that she can't go back to that, instead her eyes filled with tears at the mere thought of that.

Poor little wounded black girl with the x marked on her back from master's whip and the pretty brown skin that covered her like that.

Eyes so innocent now filled with such pain as she grabs ahold of a time once before the trauma took place as the memories fade and she tries to erase the hurt that has taken over her heart and has her bitter, angry, and mad.

Mad at the world, mad at herself, mad at the man, mad at the mom, mad at the dad, and everyone else, damn that's sad.

Her scars far deeper than the iron collar that penetrates the skin on her neck, numb from the thought of more pain.

She shuts down and daydreams while the whip cuts another x on the spot that use to be the perfect shade of black. X marks the spot where love use to be. X marks the spot where she once ruled over thee.

THE GOD IN YOU

The very first moment that I held you in my arms I knew that you had been chosen for a time such as this. A man no longer a boy carrying around the spiritual torch lite by the Holy One. Draped in the finest of blessings guided by the Divinity of Essence.

A child whom from the very start did what was required to make his mark. Transitioned from Holy to Holy. Walking with the gift of true glory.

I anticipate the rest of your story written before your entrance into this world, see you are the rarest of all gems. One of a kind totally different from any other mind. You my dear has a chosen path to an eternal blissful journey not known to any other man. God blessed you from the very start with love, compassion, and a loving caring heart.

Know that you are on the right road to receive your reward which has nothing to do with silver nor gold. It is an eternal oneness with your Spirit never before told.

The God in You is about to behold the boy turned man, carrying his Spirit in his flesh, is about to break free and show the world who he is about to be.

Complete oneness is what I grant to thee.

RELEASED

As my mind drifts into an area usually untapped. I gaze into my spirit at this unclaimed map. It's filled with all sorts of things, but one in particular a LOVE never before seen.

A LOVE that has surpassed the era of time, marked by signals of an eternal kind. My soul has claimed this priceless treasure of rare and unique pleasure.

Released by a key of everlasting unity of my spirit untold. Grab ahold of my heart and never let go. Connected by our spirits from deep within. LOVING from the third dimension, transformed by GOD'S kin.

Made for me and I for you, released by GOD to reunite us in a cue. A cue called this world tapped into our minds, led together by our spiritual maps, controlled by no mankind.

A union released by God from above, created with splendor and unforsaken LOVE. Controlled by a signal of spirit depth. Trying to hide from the world this unspoken rift. While our LOVE radiates from this spiritual cliff.

A LOVE so clear and yet unseen. Packed with a punch of terror as if in a dream. Magnetized by all that I am. While cleaving to all that you are. Searching depths never near, always those afar.

Our LOVE rare as unimagined magic from unearthly dimensions. Transformed by GOD'S clearest intentions. Released by spiritual directions while clinging to GOD'S connections.

Come LOVE me like never before throughout eternity and forevermore Priceless treasure guided to me by a spiritual map, etched in my heart directly from heaven.

Hold my hand my specially made man who will always show me from the map of especially made plans. Released by LOVE because I know that I am.

Also available for purchase on Amazon, Kindle and other online outlets:

Print and Electronic Books:

EL SHADDAI

POETICALLY ME

Electronic Books French Edition

EL SHADDAI

POETICALLY ME

Compact Disk and Electronic Play:

FOR TRUE

All Written By

VICTORIA AMIDOU

Listen to
Victoria Amidou
on:
Amazon
Google play
Jango
iheart radio
iTunes
Spotify
YouTube

www.ingramcontent.com/pod-product-compliance
Lightning Source LLC
Chambersburg PA
CBHW060114170426
43198CB00010B/886